AAT

Unit 17

National Health Service:
Draft NHS Accounting Statements and Returns

Technician

Plato

Publishing Learning And Training Organisation

First Edition

Published September 1994

by

The Publishing Learning and Training Organisation (PLATO)

13 Dulwich Wood Avenue,
London, SE19 1HB

ISBN 1 899484 01 9

Printed in England by

Communications In Print plc, Basildon, Essex

We are grateful to the Association of Accounting Technicians for permission to reproduce past examination questions.

All rights reserved

©
Copyright
PLATO
1994

Table of Contents

Introduction vi

The syllabus vii

Chapter 1   **Framework of the National Health Service**
- Introduction and brief history — 1
- April 1991 reforms — 3
- Broad financing arrangements — 5
- Present organisation in the United Kingdom — 5
- April 1996 planned reforms — 7
- The finances of the National Health Service — 9

Chapter 2   **Structure, functions and services of NHS Bodies**
- The Department of Health (DH) — 11
- The Policy Board and the Management Executive — 12
- Regional Health Authorities (RHAs) — 12
- District Health Authorities (DHAs) — 13
- Directly managed units (DMUs) — 14
- Common services — 15
- National Health Service Trusts (NHS Trusts) — 16
- General Practitioner (GP) Fundholders — 16
- Health Commissions — 18
- The role of the Director of Finance — 19
- Core values — 20

Chapter 3   **Central government funding/NHSE controls**
- Introduction — 25
- National fund allocations — 26
- Revenue allocations to RHAs — 27
- Revenue allocations to Districts and GP Fundholders — 27
- FHS allocations — 28
- Capital allocations — 28
- Joint finance — 29
- Audit arrangements — 29
- Value for money initiatives — 31
- Corporate Governance in the NHS — 32

Chapter 4   **The NHS Accounting Environment**
- Introduction and overview — 35
- The Accounting Framework — 37
- Financial directions — 43
- Standing orders — 43
- Standing financial instructions — 43
- Financial control procedures — 43
- Internal audit — 44

Chapter 5	**National Health Service Trusts**		
	Introduction	47	
	Revenue and pricing	48	
	Originating capital debt	48	
	Asset valuation	49	
	Borrowing and debt repayment	49	
	Business planning process	50	
	External Financing Limits	51	
	Financial duties	51	
Chapter 6	**Financial and business planning**		
	National planning framework	57	
	The role of regional health authorities	58	
	Directly managed units	58	
	District health authorities	59	
	Family Health Service Authorities	59	
	NHS Trust business plans	59	
	Preparation of a business case	60	
Chapter 7	**Capital expenditure and capital charges**		
	Introduction and objectives	63	
	Scope and definition	63	
	Valuation of assets and asset lives	64	
	Capital charges calculations – depreciation and interest	65	
	Impact on resource allocation and pricing for contracts	65	
	Accounting for capital charges	66	
Chapter 8	**The contracting process**		
	Introduction and types of contract	73	
	Payment arrangements	74	
	Financial control	75	
	Regionally led contracting	76	
Chapter 9	**Costing and pricing**		
	Introduction and principles	77	
	Costing techniques	78	
	Cost allocation framework	79	
	Establishing total costs	79	
	Levels of service	80	
	Cost attribution	80	
	Cost classification and analysis	81	
	National Steering Group on Costing (NSGC)	82	
	Unit costing	82	
	Performance indicators	85	

Chapter 10	**Final accounts and returns**		
	Introduction		87
	Annual accounts and financial returns		87
	Income and expenditure accounts		88
	Balance sheets		90
	Cash flow statement		91
	Supporting notes		91
	Financial returns		93
	Annual accounts in practice		94
	Statements of Standard Accounting Practice		100
	Memorandum trading accounts		101
Chapter 11	**Charitable (trust) funds**		
	Definition		103
	Powers		103
	Property and investments		103
	Income and expenditure		104
	Management		104
	Charitable funds accounts		104
	Investments		105
	Trust fund accounts		106
	NHS Charity review – Charities Act 1992		108
Chapter 12	**Glossary of NHS financial terminology**		109
Questions	1	West Health Authority	113
	2	Adun, Baran and Clede	115
	3	Central Health Authority	116
	4	Laundry	118
	5	Chubb Health Authority	120
	6	Eastern Health Authority	121
	7	East Grant Health Unit	122
	8	Reed Health Authority	124

Answers to questions available looseleaf

Introduction

Plato is a new independent organisation providing quality training and reference material for accountancy students and practitioners.

Our material is written to the highest standard by practitioners and academics who are expert in each subject.

We have identified the AAT public sector route to qualification as being of growing importance as greater financial accountability and commercial discipline are increasingly required in this area.

This book covers the essential elements of the National Health Service associated with Unit 17 of the AAT Technician Stage Course. (It does not include Limited Company Financial Statements which is extensively covered in other publications.)

While aimed primarily at the student, this publication is also intended to be an important reference book for other people, particularly health service employees and those working in other organisations who deal with the NHS who wish to gain a better understanding of how health service finance works.

The final chapter contains a number of past examination questions for students to practise on. The answers are published in separate looseleaf form to enable maximum flexibility in the use of the material by lecturers and students alike.

We will be publishing further sets of revision questions and answers and we will also regularly update the information contained in this book – as and when new laws, regulations, standards and practices come into effect.

The Syllabus

The lead body for accounting in its publication 'Standards of Competence for Accounting (Levels 2-4)' of February 1992 indicated a need for a knowledge and understanding of the following issues in connection with Unit 17.2. The following table lists those issues and indicates where they are principally dealt with in the text.

Additional issues	**Chapter**
The organisation and administration of public sector health services in the UK	1, 2
The financing and financial control of public sector health services	3, 4
The definition and valuation of assets, methods of depreciation and charging for assets	7
The operation of internal and external markets for health care	8
Statements of standard accounting practice within the Health Service, general principles and use for reference purposes	10

1

Framework of the National Health Service

Introduction and brief history

The NHS was founded in 1948 to provide health care to all citizens of the United Kingdom, regardless of their ability to pay. The principles of the NHS were outlined in the 1944 Beveridge report, 'Social Insurance and Allied Services' and then developed into legislation through the *NHS Act 1946*.

The principle that 'medical treatment and care should be made available to rich and poor alike in accordance with medical need and by no other criteria' was reaffirmed in the *National Health Services Act 1977* which defines in broad terms the objectives of the National Health Service:

'It is the Secretary of State's duty to continue the promotion of a comprehensive health service designed to secure improvement

- in the physical and mental health of the people, and

- in the prevention, diagnosis and treatment of illness,

and for that purpose to provide or secure the effective provision of services in accordance with this Act.

The services so provided shall be free of charge except in so far as the making and recovery of charges is expressly provided for by or under any enactment whenever passed.'

The National Health Service 1948-1974

The present organisation of the National Health Service has grown from three essentially separate areas of the Service which existed between 1948 and 1974. These could be summarised as follows:

- *Local authorities* were responsible for the provision of local health and school health services, which were collectively referred to as community health services. These services included such items as health centres, home nursing, vaccination and immunisation, ambulances and school clinics. The revenue cost was met out of local authorities' rate income, together with a central government contribution known as the Rate Support Grant.

- *Hospital authorities* were responsible for by far the largest element of the total National Health Service expenditure in providing for the whole range of institutionally-based hospital and specialist services. Finance for these services was provided in the form of an annually fixed allocation determined by the Department of Health and Social Security.

- *Executive councils* administered and paid for the services of family practitioners, ie. doctors, dentists, pharmacists and opticians, apart from the cost of the executive councils' own administration, for which the Department provided an annually fixed allocation. The cost of services provided by family practitioners was not subject to any predetermined ceiling.

The Health Service underwent major structural changes upon local government reorganisation in 1974 which unified the three branches, and placed them under the control of the new health authorities. This structure was modified further in 1980 in England and Wales. The 1980 changes were preceded by a Royal Commission which reported in 1979 and which had been given the following terms of reference:

> 'To consider, for the whole of the UK, in the interests both of the patients and of those who work in the NHS the best use and management of the financial and manpower resources of the NHS.' (Cmnd 7615)

The government's response to the Royal Commission was set out in a consultative paper *Patients First*. The paper deliberately emphasised that the needs of patients must be paramount. This emphasis was also made in the Royal Commission report, which had set out what it believed would be generally accepted objectives for the NHS, bearing in mind both the original philosophy of the service and the political differences that occur in its interpretation.

The National Health Service from April 1974

After 1 April 1974 a more integrated approach to the provision and financing of health care was adopted. The new Health Authorities were made responsible for the provision and integration of all community, hospital and family practitioner services within their areas, and the total cost of these services covered by an annual allocation determined by the Department of Health and Social Security with one significant exception. The family practitioner services were administered by a separate Family Practitioner Committee, independent of the Health Authority, but having a small degree of common membership. The services themselves continue to operate under an 'open ended' budget. This meant that whereas the hospital and community services had to provide health care facilities within a pre-determined financial limit, the family practitioner services' expenditure was reimbursed directly without any constraint in financial terms being placed upon the general practitioners, dentists, pharmacists and opticians.

Because of the substantial sums of public funds involved, the direct allocations that Health Authorities received carried significant controls and limitations on their use. The duties and responsibilities of Health Authorities, which they exercised as agents of the Secretary of State, were decided by statute and this limited the purposes for which expenditure could be incurred. However, the principle of free access to health care facilities for the whole population continued to be the cornerstone of all legislation covering the National Health Service.

Health Service Act 1980

The present structure of the NHS was established by the *Health Service Act 1980* and became operative in 1982. In England the NHS was organised as a three-tier administrative structure. In

Scotland, Wales and Northern Ireland there were only two tiers. In recent years, the NHS has undergone considerable structural development, most notably the establishment of the Policy Board and the Management Executive, together with the recommendations of the 1989 White Paper *Working for Patients* affecting the structure and constitution of health authorities, dealt with in Chapter 2.

April 1991 reforms

In January 1989, the Government published a White Paper *Working for Patients* which proposed wide ranging reforms of the NHS. These reforms were to secure the following key changes (and subsequently became the *National Health Service and Community Care Act 1990*).

- To make the Health Service more responsive to the needs of patients, as much power and responsibility as possible would be delegated to local level.

- To stimulate a better service to the patient, hospitals would be able to apply for new self-governing status as NHS Hospital Trusts.

- To enable hospitals which best meet the needs and wishes of patients to get the money to do so, the money required to treat patients would be able to cross administrative boundaries.

- To reduce waiting times and improve the quality of service, to help give the individual patients appointment times they can rely on, and to help cut the long hours worked by some junior doctors, 100 new consultant posts would be created over the next three years.

- To help the family doctor improve service to patients, large GP practices would be able to apply for their own budgets to obtain a defined range of services direct from hospitals.

- To improve the effectiveness of NHS management, regional, district and family practitioner management bodies would be reduced in size and reformed on business lines, with executive and non-executive directors.

- To ensure that all concerned with delivering services to the patient make the best use of the resources available to them, quality of service and value for money would be more rigorously audited.

The main elements of the reforms are outlined below:

- *Managing the service*

    The NHS is to continue to be funded by government mainly from tax revenues and as such the Secretary of State for Health must be accountable to Parliament. However, wherever possible decisions on operational matters in the NHS must be taken locally by operational units, with Ministers being responsible for policy and strategy (see Chapter 3).

- *Self-governing hospitals*

    Major acute hospitals with more than 250 beds would be encouraged to become 'self-governing'. Thus hospitals would be formally vested in a new and separate legal body, to be known as an NHS Hospital Trust, run by a board of directors with a Chairman appointed by the Secretary of State. These trusts would be empowered by statute to employ staff; to enter into contracts both to provide services and to buy in services and supplies from others; and to raise income within statutory limits. The hospitals would earn the revenue by selling services to district health authorities, general practitioners, private patients, insurance companies etc. The aim was to stimulate more efficient and effective performance. The first 'wave' of self-governing hospitals were established in 1991 (see Chapter 5).

- *Funding health authorities*

  Changes were proposed to the method of centrally funding health authorities. These changes will be described in Chapter 3.

- *GP Fund Holders*

  Family doctors with over 11,000 patients would be offered budgets with which to buy hospital care and out-patient care from either NHS hospitals or the private sector and for drugs, staff and premises. See Chapters 2 and 3 for more details of these changes.

- *External audit*

  On the financial side it was proposed that the Audit Commission takes on the statutory audit of health authorities and also 'value for money' studies in the NHS. Audit arrangements are dealt with in more detail in Chapter 3.

- *Community care and local authorities*

  For many years, community care had been the subject of much criticism mainly due to the ineffective national and regional planning, as well as to wide variations in provision by local authorities and health authorities. The government issued a White Paper in October 1989 entitled *Caring for People*, which identified that local authorities should take the lead role in community care. The main elements of the White Paper were:

  - local authorities should be given the lead role in community care planning, but should conduct their planning exercises in close co-operation with District Health Authorities (DHAs) and Family Health Service Authorities (FHSAs);

  - users should no longer have to 'fit in' to existing services, but rather services need to be redesigned to meet user needs which have been uncovered by new multi-disciplinary assessment systems;

  - budgets should be devolved as close to the user as possible to allow flexible, local purchasing; a 'care management' system is seen as the preferred way to obtain user-sensitive provision;

  - local authorities to assume more of an enabling role through the allocation of funds, but a declining role in service provision; instead, services were to be increasingly provided by a mixed economy of care based largely upon the private and voluntary sectors;

  - the transfer to local social services authorities of the care element of social security income support currently paid to residents of private and voluntary residential and nursing homes; local authorities would have discretion on how to use this funding.

These proposals were enacted through the *NHS and Community Care Act 1990* with a view to implementation in April 1991. But soon after the passage of the Act, the government announced an implementation delay on the ground that local authorities were not sufficiently prepared for the changes. Some took the view that a more pertinent reason for the delay was concern about the local authority expenditure implications at a time of high sensitivity about poll tax levels.

Instead, it was decided that implementation would be spread over three years, commencing in April 1991. The timetable has been as follows:

- April 1991: inspection units and complaints procedures to be established by local authorities; first availability of specific grants for mental illness and for drug and alcohol abuse;

- April 1992: the first community care plans to be produced by local authorities, DHAs and FHSAs;

- April 1993: new assessment procedures to be in place; social security income support to be transferred to social services authorities; realignment of commissioning and providing roles within social services departments;

- onwards: development of care management and new service patterns based on the assessment of individual needs.

A consequence of these important structural changes was the creation of an 'internal market' in the NHS, with purchasers and providers negotiating contracts to provide the best types of health care within the overall cash limited sums available.

Broad financing arrangements

The NHS is funded partly out of employer's and employees' National Insurance Contributions, but mainly from general taxation. Some diagnostic services and treatments are free to patients requiring them. For other items such as spectacles, dentistry and drugs prescribed by GPs, most patients bear at least part of the cost, but there are important exemptions. Recent governments have introduced charges for certain previously free items such as eye tests, though NHS consultations with GPs and specialists, as well as NHS hospital treatment, remain free.

The National Health Service is therefore almost wholly dependent upon central government funding. Unlike local government, it has no independent source of revenue equivalent to business rates or the community charge, but instead its finances are determined by the Cabinet in the annual public expenditure allocation process. Health authorities can raise limited amounts of money by fund-raising activities.

Present organisation in the United Kingdom

The National Health Service in England is now organised into:

- 14 Regional Health Authorities in England primarily responsible for strategy;

- approximately 160 District Health Authorities responsible for purchasing services for their residents;

- approximately 600 'Directly Managed Units' responsible for providing services on contract to District Health Authorities.

Also from April 1991, 57 Units became legal entities known as Self-Governing Trusts. Their accountability is direct to the Secretary of State. Further waves of Trusts have been established annually since then.

Each statutory authority has 10 members: 5 Executive (General Manager and Finance Director being mandatory), and 5 Non-Executive plus a Chairperson appointed by the Secretary of State.

The present structure in England

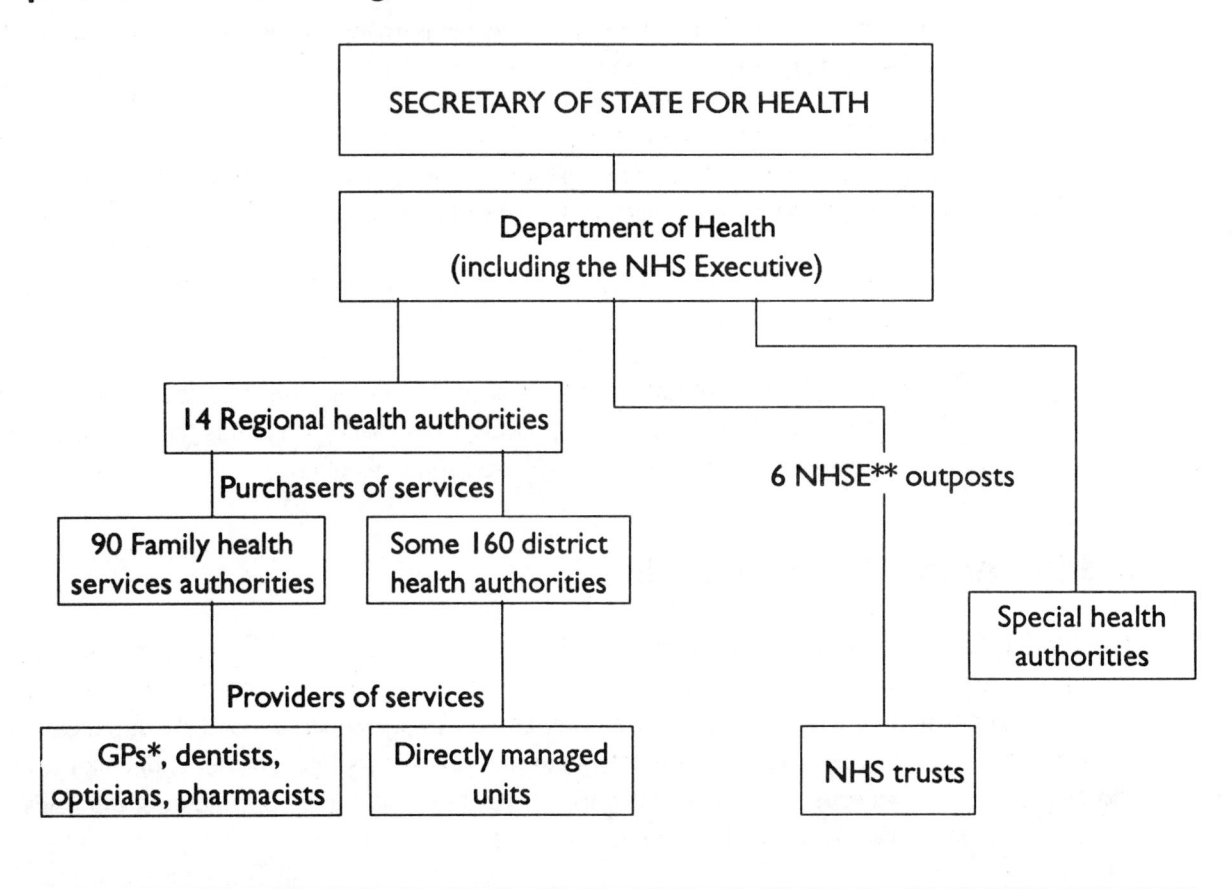

```
                    SECRETARY OF STATE FOR HEALTH
                                 │
                    Department of Health
                    (including the NHS Executive)
                    │                           │
        14 Regional health authorities          │
            Purchasers of services      6 NHSE** outposts
        ┌───────────────┬───────────────┐       │
   90 Family health    Some 160 district         │
   services authorities  health authorities    Special health
        │               │                      authorities
            Providers of services
        ┌───────────────┬───────────────┐
   GPs*, dentists,     Directly managed    NHS trusts
   opticians, pharmacists    units
```

* Some GPs are Fundholders (see Chapter 2)

** NHSE stands for National Health Service Executive, formerly known as National Health Service Management Executive (NHSME)

The position in the rest of the United Kingdom is:

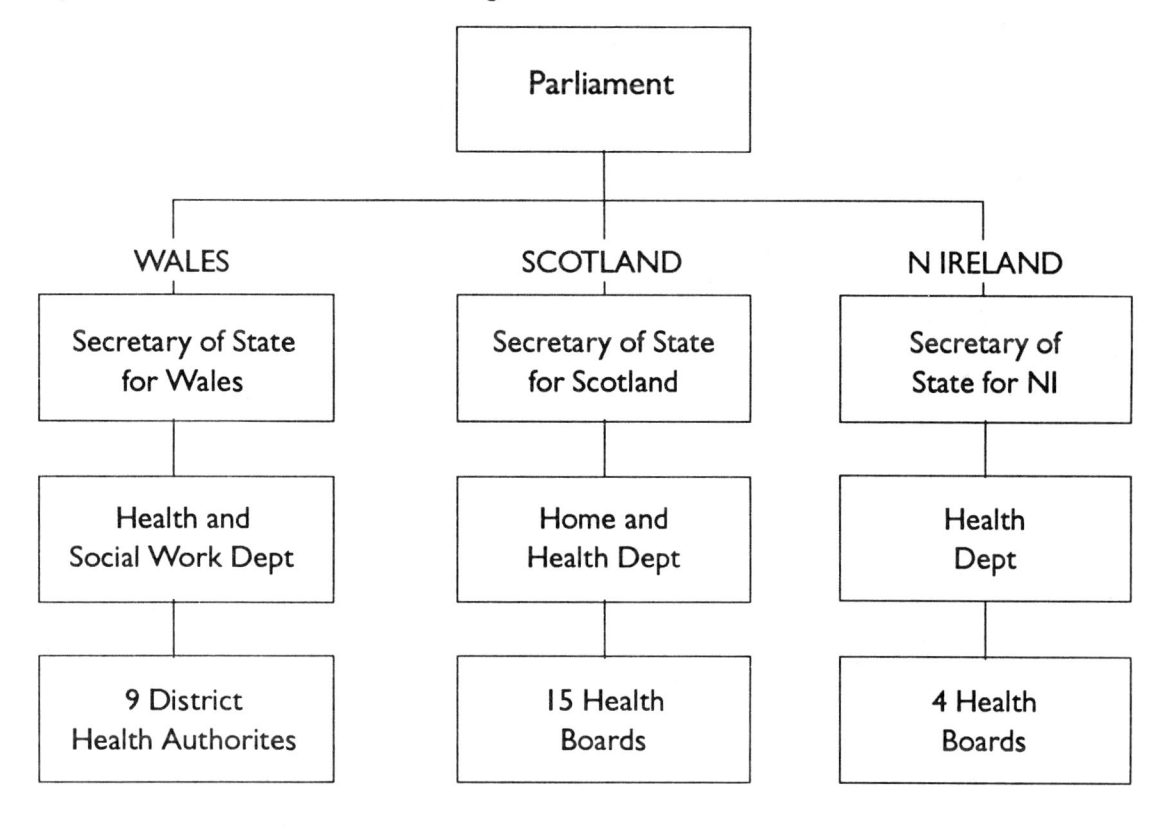

```
                        ┌──────────────┐
                        │  Parliament  │
                        └──────┬───────┘
        ┌──────────────────────┼──────────────────────┐
      WALES                 SCOTLAND                N IRELAND
┌──────────────┐      ┌──────────────────┐      ┌──────────────┐
│ Secretary of │      │  Secretary of    │      │  Secretary of│
│ State for    │      │  State for       │      │  State for NI│
│ Wales        │      │  Scotland        │      │              │
└──────┬───────┘      └────────┬─────────┘      └──────┬───────┘
┌──────┴───────┐      ┌────────┴─────────┐      ┌──────┴───────┐
│ Health and   │      │  Home and        │      │  Health      │
│ Social Work  │      │  Health Dept     │      │  Dept        │
│ Dept         │      │                  │      │              │
└──────┬───────┘      └────────┬─────────┘      └──────┬───────┘
┌──────┴───────┐      ┌────────┴─────────┐      ┌──────┴───────┐
│ 9 District   │      │  15 Health       │      │  4 Health    │
│ Health       │      │  Boards          │      │  Boards      │
│ Authorites   │      │                  │      │              │
└──────────────┘      └──────────────────┘      └──────────────┘
```

April 1996 planned reforms

This position, however, will be short-lived as radical reorganisation plans were announced in Parliament on 21 October 1993 by the Secretary of State for Health.

They include:

- the abolition of the 14 statutory RHAs and the reorganisation of the NHSE to include eight regional offices – each headed by a regional director – to replace both the RHAs and the existing NHSE outposts;

- the creation of a clear identity for the NHS Executive, within the Department of Health, as the 'headquarters of the NHS';

- the appointment of non-executive members to the NHS Policy Board to cover each of the eight new regions thereby providing a link between ministers and local DHA, FHSA and trust chairmen; and

- enabling DHAs and FHSAs to merge to create stronger local purchasers with such mergers being encouraged actively.

Timing

As a first step towards the new structure, the government merged the existing RHAs into eight new interim regional health authorities from 1 April 1994. The boundaries of the eight new RHAs would match those of the eight newly-created regional offices of the NHSE.

A consultation document on RHA mergers was published on 1 November 1993 and bodies consulted had until 15 January 1994 to respond.

Legislation is needed in order to abolish RHAs and to enable DHAs and FHSAs to merge. The aim is to achieve this in the 1994/95 parliamentary session, with the abolition of authorities taking effect on 1 April 1996.

Regional directors took up posts from 1 April 1994 as members of a restructured NHS Executive. Selected individuals are also acting as regional general managers of the transitional RHAs, retaining responsibility for residual RHA functions.

The regional offices of the NHSE will also began operating from 1 April 1994, incorporating the functions of the existing NHSE outposts.

Functions

It is recognised that RHAs have played an important role in NHS management for many years and the decision to abolish them has not been taken lightly. However, the development of the NHS reforms has already brought about a shift of responsibility towards local purchasers and providers and it is considered that there is no longer a need for 14 separate statutory bodies at an intermediate level.

The new NHSE regional offices will take on those functions of the RHAs which remain the responsibility of central management. They will be responsible for developing the purchasing function and primary care within the health service and will also take over the task of monitoring NHS trusts from the existing NHSE outposts.

The functions of the regional offices in relation to purchasers and providers will be kept clear and distinct. The regional offices will provide a link between strategic and local management; they will not become involved in detailed operational matters which are the responsibility of local health authorities and trusts.

The regional offices will be much smaller than the present RHAs and will employ fewer staff. The total staffing budget for each office will be set when the allocation of functions across the new structure has been finalised and these limits will be adhered to rigorously. A similar overall limit will be set for the NHSE as a whole.

The functions of the eight NHSE regional offices will be:

- ensuring compliance with the regulatory framework of the internal market;
- managing the performance of both purchasers and providers;
- arbitration on disputes;
- approving GP fundholder applications and budgets;
- purchaser development; targeted contributions to central work on policy and resources;
- working with the professions;
- working with universities;
- public health;
- aspects of human resource management.

The finances of the National Health Service

In 1992/93, total spending on the NHS was in excess of £34.4 billion. At 1949 prices spending has doubled from £400 million to about £800 million.

As a percentage of gross domestic product, NHS spending in the United Kingdom since 1980/81 has broadly moved as follows:

	%	
1980/81	5.0	
1981/82	5.1,	then a gradual decline to ...
1989/90	4.75,	then a gradual increase to ...
1992/93	5.5	

Although taxation has always been the main source of NHS finance since its inception, there has been an overall reduction in the burden on general taxpayers, as other sources of finance have emerged. A summary of the position at 10-year intervals shows:

	Taxation %	NHS contributions %	Local health authorities %	Patients %
1949	100.0	–	–	–
1959	73.6	13.7	8.6	4.1
1969	78.8	10.4	7.3	3.6
1979	88.3	9.5	–	2.2
1989	80.8	16.1	–	2.1
1993	82.9	14.2	–	3.0

Allocating NHS finance

For the purposes of revenue distribution, the NHS is divided into two parts:

- the hospital and community health services (HCHS);

- family health services (FHS).

HCHS covers district health authorities, while the FHS includes general practitioners, dentists, opticians and pharmacists. GP fundholders are allocated their own budgets direct, with which to purchase health care on behalf of their patients. About 75% of the total NHS budget is allocated to HCH services on a cash-limited basis, via the regional health authorities. RHA allocations are designed to meet specific regional needs and problems. Subsequent allocations are made on broadly similar considerations.

Structure, functions and services of NHS Bodies

The Department of Health (DH)

Responsible to Parliament is the Secretary of State for Health, aided by Ministers for Health. These Ministers are served by the civil servants of the Department of Health and the NHS Executive.

The *National Health Service Act 1977* sets out the powers and duties of the Secretary of State. The principal duties are 'to continue the promotion in England and Wales of a comprehensive health service designed to secure improvement:

- in the physical and mental health of the people of those countries; and
- in the prevention, diagnosis and treatment of illness,

and for that purpose to provide or secure the effective provision of services in accordance with this Act.

The services so provided shall be free except in so far as the making and recovery of charges is expressly provided for by or under any enactment, whenever passed.'

It is the Secretary of State's duty to provide throughout England and Wales, to such extent as is considered necessary to meet all reasonable requirements:

- hospital accommodation;
- medical, dental, nursing and ambulance services;
- facilities for the care of expectant and nursing mothers and young children as is considered appropriate;
- facilities for the prevention of illness, the care of persons suffering from illness, and after-care of persons who have suffered from illness, as is considered appropriate;
- other services as are required for the diagnosis and treatment of illness.

The key functions of the Secretary of State and the Department of Health are centred on establishing national plans, priorities and policies for the NHS and monitoring how successfully such policies are implemented by the lower tiers of the NHS. Thus the Secretary of State is continually monitoring the efficiency and effectiveness of the lower tiers. Having established plans and priorities it is the Secretary of State's responsibility to obtain a share of the national resources to administer the NHS and distribute these resources throughout the country in order that the plans will be achieved. The mechanisms for distribution are discussed in Chapter 3. It is mandatory for health authorities to keep their drawings within the approved cash limit plus any additional income which can be generated locally. Monthly returns of key financial figures are made to the NHSE.

The Policy Board and the Management Executive

The Secretary of State announced that from 1989 two bodies would assist the Secretary in the national planning and management of the NHS: (i) the Policy Board and (ii) the NHS (Management) Executive. . The Policy Board comprises the Secretary of State and appointed members from industry, and is responsible for determining the strategy, objectives and finances of the NHS in the light of government policy.

It sets objectives for the Management Executive which has responsibility for the operation and management of the NHS within the framework set by ministers and the Policy Board. It informs the Policy Board of resource needs, proposes distribution of funds to regions, and deals with pay and personnel issues. It is also responsible for setting health authorities' objectives and monitoring them through regional planning and review processes. The members of the Management Executive Board are appointed by the Secretary of State, headed by a Chief Executive and supported by officers responsible for specific functions such as finance, personnel and nursing. Its membership is drawn from the NHS, Civil Service and the private sector.

Regional Health Authorities (RHAs)

In England at second tier level there are currently 14 Regional Health Authorities which cover geographical areas extending over several local authority boundaries.

Regional Health Authorities interpret the policies of the Department of Health and draw up policies which suit the particular needs of their regions in regional strategic plans. These plans are produced after consultation with the third tier of the NHS, the District Health Authorities. The plans attempt to assess the health care pattern for particular regions over the following ten-year period. The regional strategic plan must be submitted to the Department of Health for approval.

When approved, the plans will form the basis of health care policy over a period of time and subject to an annual review. Each Regional Health Authority is responsible for allocating the funds, received from the Department of Health, to the District Health Authorities within the Region. These funds will be allocated in a way which will allow the regional strategic plan to be achieved. It is each Region's responsibility to then subsequently monitor the expenditure of its District Health Authorities.

Regions give advice to the Districts on policy implementation and are directly responsible for managing some services, on a region wide basis, so that the benefits of economies of scale may accrue. In many cases, these regional services eg. ambulances, blood transfusion, information technology are either provided by Trusts, or by the private sector.

Structure and role of Regional Health Authorities

The RHA as a governing body consists of 10 members plus a chairman appointed by the Secretary of State for Health (see Chapter 1, page 5: 'Present organisation in the United Kingdom').

The RHA is responsible for strategic planning and controlling the health service for the patients living in its geographical area. It receives the revenue and capital cash limit for the region and is responsible for allocating it between itself and the DHAs in the manner it sees most appropriate. Broadly speaking it will operate the same rules for cash limits as are operated by the DH, ie. allocation according to population, with the same carry-over and virement rules for revenue and capital cash limits.

However, the RHA is free to vary these rules and may for instance give a DHA a very large capital allocation in one year to allow a large capital project to be completed with a consequential reduction in future years. The responsibility for all the DHAs and RHAs to keep within the regional cash limits lies with the RHA.

The RHA is also responsible for allocating the proceeds from the sale of any fixed assets used by DHAs in its region to the DHAs. The DH has required that this be operated in such a way that DHAs who sell the assets they use benefit from the sale, but ultimately this distribution is the responsibility of the RHA.

The requirement of hospitals and community health service to pay capital charges to the RHA for the assets that they use has been introduced by the *NHS and Community Care Act 1990* and came into effect on 1 April 1991. As already stated, these charges are paid to the RHA who may allocate the proceeds to the DHAs for revenue expenditure as they see fit. For further details of capital charges – see Chapter 7.

If a DHA has a capital scheme costing over £5m this will be carried out by the RHA on behalf of the DHA and all accounting entries relating to such schemes will appear in the books of the RHA until the scheme is complete. The scheme is then transferred from the RHA to the DHA in the accounts of the appropriate Directly Managed Unit (see page 14).

District Health Authorities (DHAs)

There are about 160 District Health Authorities in England. These authorities are responsible for providing hospital and community health services, through Directly Managed Units (DMUs), but with the introduction of the internal market and, especially, of NHS trusts, the DHA is moving to become the purchaser of health care services from other bodies. Thus the DHAs are the providers of health services in line with policies set at a national and regional level. It is at the District level that health needs are identified and fed back into the planning systems of the Department of Health and the Region. It is Districts' responsibility to identify service deficiencies and to apply to the Regions for funds to meet such deficiencies or to cut existing services or find other economies. The funds allocated by the Regions to DHAs are based on such indicators of need as population, demography (ie. population structure), and various health and cost indicators. This will be explained more fully in Chapter 3.

Structure and function of DHAs

The DHA as a governing body consists of a chairman appointed by the Secretary of State for Health and 10 other members (see Chapter 1, page 5: 'Present organisation in the United Kingdom').

The NHS and Community Care Act 1990 provided that from 1 April 1991, the role of the DHA in planning the services to be provided was separated from their role of administering and managing the provision of hospital and community services.

This means that the DHAs now have two separate roles, as a *purchaser* of services and as a *provider* of services. As a purchaser of services the DHA receives a revenue allocation from the RHA and decides which services are required for the population living in their area. It then enters into contracts with the following bodies to purchase the services required.

- Directly Managed Units (see page 14)

- NHS Trust hospitals (see Chapter 5)

- Private sector hospitals and services.

These contracts, which are an important part of the internal market, do not have the legal status of normal contracts and if a dispute arises in connection with them, the Secretary of State or his/her representative acts as arbiter. Contracting is further considered in Chapter 8.

Some people living in a district will be patients of general practitioners who are budget-holders. In these cases it is the general practitioners and not the DHA who receive an allocation of funds and are responsible for purchasing the health care required by their patients (see page 16: 'General Practitioner (GP) Fundholders').

The DHA also receives a capital allocation from the RHA and is required to allocate this among the services they are responsible for, according to their plans for the service. Although the amount of the revenue and capital allocation is decided by the RHA the actual cash is requisitioned directly from the DH by the DHA.

Directly managed units (DMUs)

Under the NHS and Community Care Act 1990, all the hospital and community services previously run by the DHA are required to be organised into a number of Directly Managed Units (DMUs). These are managed as separate entities which decide on which services they can provide, and the price of these services. They also keep separate accounts which show the surplus or deficit achieved by the activities of the DMU. The units are under the control of the DHA and their accounts are consolidated with those of the DHA.

Some hospitals and community services which were previously run by the DHA have now become NHS trusts and are thus self-governing and responsible directly to the NHSE outposts.

The major source of income of a DMU is the payment it receives from the DHA for the provision of services. This is paid by the DHA out of its revenue allocation from the RHA.

DMUs have limited powers to carry out income-generating schemes and are also empowered to provide services to non-NHS patients and receive money from this source. Units may also receive donations for both revenue and capital expenditure and this will be recorded in the first instance in the charitable (Trust) Fund's accounts, which is a separate set of accounts for recording donations (see Chapter 11). When it is transferred to the DMU it will be recorded in their accounts as income.

If fixed assets have been purchased from donations, they will be recorded in the accounts of the DMU in such a way that the DMU will not have to pay capital charges on these to the RHA. The reason for this is that it is considered appropriate that the DMU receiving such donations should be able to benefit from them rather than their benefit reverting to the RHA. Fixed assets are also purchased from the capital allocation of the DHA but generally the financing of these assets will appear in the accounts of the DHA and when they are purchased, these assets will be transferred to the books of the DMU.

Common services

There may be certain activities which were in the past carried out by the DHA, such as payroll or laundry services and which are now used by a number of DMUs and possibly the DHA in its purchaser role as well. These are called *common services*, and it is now necessary for separate accounts to be kept for these services. These accounts will be kept in precisely the same way as those for DMUs, and will be consolidated with those of the DHA. The only difference is that the revenue income will be the 'internal market' payments made by other sections for the use of their services.

The following paragraphs, from the 1993 year book of the National Association of Health Authorities and Trusts, provide additional information on key aspects of the present NHS organisation.

'Family Health Services Authorities (FHSAs)

FHSAs exist to manage the services provided by GPs, dentists, retail pharmacists and opticians. These family practitioners are independent contractors and not NHS employees. The terms and conditions under which they work are negotiated nationally between the health professions and the government. FHSAs are responsible for implementing the national contracts in their areas.

As a result of the NHS reforms, emanating from the *1990 NHS and Community Care Act*, the role of FHSAs has been strengthened and they are now much more actively involved than hitherto in planning the development of services in their areas.

For historical reasons, the boundaries of FHSAs differed from those of DHAs. There are 90 FHSAs in England serving populations which range from 130,000 to 1,600,000, but boundaries are now becoming aligned with those of DHAs.

Each authority comprises a chairman appointed by the Secretary of State, five lay non-executive members and four professional non-executives (a GP, dentist, pharmacist and community nurse) appointed by the RHA, and a general manager. The functions of FHSAs include:

- managing the contracts of family practitioners;
- paying practitioners in accordance with their contracts;
- providing information to the public;
- dealing with complaints from the public;
- allocating funds for GP practice developments.

Family practitioners retain considerable influence over the running of services. An important channel of influence for GPs is the local medical committee. This committee is elected by GPs in each area to express the views of GPs to FHSAs. The local medical committee operates alongside similar committees for other family practitioners.

National Health Service Trusts (NHS Trusts)

NHS trusts were first established in 1991 under the NHS reforms. The function of trusts is to provide hospital and community services on behalf of the Secretary of State. Trusts are self-governing units, with their own boards of directors and with freedom to organise their own affairs, subject only to the legal framework within which they operate, and the contracts they have negotiated with purchasers.

The performance of trusts is monitored by the NHS Executive outposts. Each trust is required to prepare an annual business plan outlining, among other things, its proposals for service developments and capital investment. This is examined by the management executive outpost to ensure the trust meets its financial responsibilities.

The main financial duties of trusts are:

- to break even;

- to earn a 6% return on their capital;

- to contain capital expenditure within the external financing limit set by the Secretary of State.

Outposts of the management executive monitor financial performance in trusts on a regular basis to ensure that they meet financial targets. Outposts also review the published annual reports and accounts of trusts to check that financial duties have been fulfilled.

The number of trusts is increasing as the NHS reforms continue to be implemented. There is an annual cycle of applications for trust status and it is anticipated that most if not all NHS services will be run as trusts by 1995. When this happens, there will be a complete separation of purchaser and provider roles. Further details of NHS Trusts are contained in Chapter 5.

General Practitioner (GP) Fundholders

The introduction of General Practice Fundholding is one of the major developments in the NHS and reflects the General Practitioner's position as one of the purchasers of health services.

The initiative was introduced in order to give the practitioner and hence his or her patient, the ability, within the finance available, to exercise a greater freedom of choice.

Subject to a minimum practice list size and subject to ability to manage funds practices may opt to become fundholders. In doing so the doctors within the practice are empowered to contract with the hospital or unit of their choice for certain treatments and services and to decide whether or not the money allocated is to be applied to drugs, hospital or community health services, or other forms of care.

The 'fund' is allocated to the practice by the RHA and comprises three parts: practice staff reimbursement, applicable hospital and community health services and drugs. Whilst the fund is allocated under the three headings in the first instance, the practitioner is able to transfer money from one heading to another and to carry forward savings from one year to another. Savings may then be spent on further services.

GP practices that are accepted as fundholders are responsible for purchasing a defined range of services for their patients. These services include:

- selective non-emergency in-patient and day case treatments;
- out-patient services;
- domiciliary visits;
- direct access tests and investigations (pathology, radiology, audiology);
- direct access therapy (physio, occupational, speech, dietetics, chiropody);
- community health services, including eg. nursing and health visiting services;
- drugs;
- employment of practice staff.

Other services are purchased for patients of GP fundholders by their DHAs.

Originally, it was anticipated that only practices with 11,000 or more registered patients would become fundholders. This limit has since been reduced by the government and encouragement has been given to smaller practices to apply for fundholding status. FHSAs are gradually assuming responsibility on behalf of RHAs for administering fundholding and monitoring the use of resources by GP fundholders.

The resources allocated to fundholding practices are deducted from the allocation of the relevant District Health Authorities. It is the government's aim to move to a funding formula in which the money fundholders receive is based on the number of patients served, adjusted for age, sex and other factors. This will replace the current funding formula, which allocates resources according to the use made of services in the past and the hospital referral patterns of GPs.

Community Health Councils (CHCs)

Community Health Councils have existed since 1974 to represent the public's interest in the NHS. They are statutory bodies, established by RHAs, and there is usually one CHC for each DHA. CHCs have no executive powers. Their main job is to advise DHAs and FHSAs on the views and concerns of patients and the public. CHCs are, in effect, patient watchdogs.

The members of CHCs are drawn from voluntary organisations, local authorities and the local community. These members are supported by a full-time secretary (or chief officer) and one or more assistant. A typical annual budget for a community health council, provided by the RHA, is around £40,000.

CHCs have interpreted their responsibilities in different ways. Some have chosen to concentrate on helping members of the public by giving advice and assistance with complaints procedures and providing information. Others have given priority to lobbying NHS authorities and trusts and mounting pressure group campaigns.

To support them in their role, Parliament has agreed that CHCs should have the following rights:

- to relevant information from NHS authorities;
- to access to certain NHS premises;
- to inclusion in consultation on substantial developments or variations in services;
- to send observers to meetings of district health authorities and family health services authorities.

Each CHC has a duty to publish an annual report and this is discussed at meetings with the DHA and FHSA.'

Health Commissions

Health Commissions work in partnership with Direct Health Authorities and FHSAs. They are separate bodies but share a common team of officers and are concerned with establishing the needs of patients in their area and ensuring that services are subsequently made available to meet those needs.

A leaflet published in 1992 by the Wessex Regional Health Authority gave details of the arrangements for the establishment, in September 1992, of health commissions in the region's area. An extract from this leaflet is set out below and indicates the scope and work of health commissions.

'North and Mid-Hampshire Health Commission

The Commission brings together Basingstoke and North Hampshire Health Authority, Winchester Health Authority and Hampshire Family Health Services Authority in a partnership to secure better health and improved health services for the 600,000 people living in central and northern Hampshire.

The geographical area covered by the Commission is very varied, stretching from Tadley in the north to Eastleigh in the south and from Andover in the west to Farnborough and Aldershot in the east. There are a number of larger urban areas like Winchester and Basingstoke, smaller market towns like Andover and Alton and, particularly on the east side of the Commission, rural areas. Aldershot also has a large military population.

Managing the Commission

The chair of the Commission is Mrs Angela Sealey, chair of Basingstoke and North Hampshire Health Authority, and the vice-chair is Mr Luke March, vice-chair of Winchester Health Authority. Both were appointed by the chair of Wessex Regional Health Authority. There are nine non-executive members of the Commission, drawn equally from the three constituent authorities of Winchester and Basingstoke DHAs and Hampshire FHSA.

The Commission, which is based in Basingstoke, has an executive team led by the chief executive, Dr Kate Barnard. Five executive directors have been appointed to the Commission and the assistant director of Social Services for north and mid-Hampshire is invited to all meetings. The three community health councils covered by north and mid-Hampshire also attend the Commission's regular meetings, all of which are held in public.

The Commission's profile

The Commission spends £250 million each year on purchasing health care for its resident population. That is about £450 for each resident – a higher level than the rest of the region enjoys.

There are:

- 312 GPs in the Commission area in 76 GP practices. Between them, GP practices in the Commission employ the equivalent of over 440 full-time staff which includes 78 practice nurses. From April 1993, 131 of all Commission GPs will be fundholders, covering more than 40% of the population.

- 198 general dental practitioners in the Commission situated in 97 practices.

- 88 chemists registered with the FHSA in 29 settlements.

- 208 opticians, many practising from more than one site.'

The role of the Director of Finance

The NHS Executive published a booklet under this title in January 1994, prepared by the Director of Finance of the Yorkshire Health Authority. The following paragraphs from the introduction to that booklet, give an atmosphere of the environment in which health finance directors are working.

'In any organisation – whether in the public or private sector – the Director of Finance is one of the most significant and important people. Working in the context of the NHS requires not just high quality professional expertise but particularly well-developed personal qualities such as integrity, strength of character and inter-personal skills.

The newly-formed NHS now operates as a developing internal market but is still constrained within finite, cash-limited resources. This makes the Directors of Finance's contribution even more vital and their mission (as with all others concerned with managing in the NHS) is to use the resources available to provide the most efficient, cost effective and best quality services possible. This must always be at the forefront.

The atmosphere of the NHS is often one which is emotionally very highly-charged. Directors of Finance need to show commitment and empathy with the objectives of the NHS. They must be able to win and retain the respect of clinicians and all the other professionals in the NHS.

As leaders in their profession, Directors of Finance need to develop leadership qualities. They need to be able to think ahead, plan effectively, shape the finance function to meet the needs of the organisation, 'build people', delegate effectively, etc.

Similarly, higher tier Directors of Finance at the NHSE or RHAs need to show exceptional leadership qualities in order to give cohesive and positive leadership to NHS Trusts, DHAs and FHSAs in the direction required by the NHS.

It is essential that Directors of Finance build a finance function which operates to extremely high standards. The basic financial and management accounting functions are vitally important in such a dynamic organisation – acute provider units are a prime example of this. If financial information is not soundly based, Directors of Finance will not be able to retain credibility within their organisations, no matter how able they are on a personal and professional basis.

There may be a rather different emphasis in terms of the skills required in a purchasing organisation, eg. on longer-term financial planning, option appraisal and forecasting. Essentially, however, the background and qualifications required are similar. In provider units 'business management' experience may be valuable and consideration should be given to how Directors of Finance could be exposed to development in this area, eg. by secondment or formal training or simply by contact with non-executives for the private sector.'

This document sets out in the appendices what are categorised as the four distinct roles of Directors of Finance:

The NHSE's vision and core values for the finance function were identified in 'Framework for the Future'. The following are quotes from Gordon Greenshield's address to the CIPFA Conference in June 1992, and set out in 'Framework for the Future'.

'Vision

To strive for and achieve a finance function which is recognised both by the NHS and the private sector as:

- being of the very highest quality which adds value to the organisation;

- being professionally sound, proactive, innovative and enterprising;

- providing an environment in which training and development, and flexible career paths are open to all.'

Quality is the foundation of the vision. We must identify our customers and their needs, and then ensure that we not only meet but exceed those needs. To do this there must be a sound professional base which encourages initiative, adopts a proactive approach and achieves high standards of planning and management.

The vision of the future is challenging but exciting. The starting point for addressing the future is to identify the required culture and establish core values which can underpin that culture.'

Core values

The core values for the finance function have been identified as:

- **Professionalism – 'Meeting the Standard'**

    Acquire and apply appropriate knowledge, skills and best practice which will enable all finance staff to meet customers' needs to consistently high standards.

- **Integrity – 'Doing the right things'**

    Act in a manner which is honest, open, impartial and fair. Our approach will be objective, consistent and reflect the highest ethical standards.

- **Partnership – 'Working together'**

    Work with others to develop mutual understanding and trust to enable the organisation to achieve its corporate objectives.

- **Innovation – 'Changing for the better'**

    Develop an environment which encourages enterprise, challenge and creativity. This will stimulate people to welcome change and manage risk."

Statutory position of the Director of Finance

The statutory duties of the Director are set out in *'Directions on Financial Management in England'* published in 1991. In summary, the responsibilities of the Board, Chief Executor and Director of Finance are:

Board

'An authority as a whole, including both executive and non-executive members, is responsible for ensuring compliance with the requirements of the Directions. It must be satisfied that sound financial management is maintained and that the cash limit is met.

Authority Standing Financial Instructions must set out the responsibilities of individual officers . . .'

General Manager

'. . .The General Manager has overall executive responsibility for the authority's activities and is responsible to the authority for ensuring that it stays within its cash limit (where it applies). He, or she, is responsible for ensuring that the authority receives financial information . . .'

Director of Finance

'. . . The Director of Finance provides the financial information and advice and is responsible for supervising the financial control and accounting systems.'

It is essential that all Directors are fully aware of and attentive to the detail of these Directions (of which the above are short extracts) and any other responsibility laid upon them by the Secretary of State, Chief Executives and Directors of Finance have a particular duty to ensure that other Directors have these matters brought to their attention.

Directors of Finance are 'prescribed officer members' of the Board (under Statutory Instrument 1990 No 1331). Therefore, they are members of the Board for as long as they fill their post.

The remainder of the booklet deals with the four main roles of the Director of Finance. These are set out below, together with the sub-headings in the case of each role, to give an indication of the issues covered.

Corporate Management role:
> Member of the Board and Management Team
> Working with Clinical Managers
> Strategic and Business Planning
> Corporate Governance
> Value for Money
> Contribution to the Internal Market
> Business Case Assessment
> Private Sector Finance
> Non-Finance Management Responsibilities

Public Accountability and Stewardship role:
> Directors of Finance in the Public Service
> Guarding Financial Instructions and Financial Control Systems
> Statutory accounts and Returns
> Financial Reporting
> Monitoring Information

Financial Management role:
> Financial Strategy
> Budgetary Control and Reporting
> Financial Accounting
> Treasury Management
> Financial Services
> Charitable Funds

Management of the Finance Directorate role:
> High Standards of Management
> Business Planning linked to the Corporate Objectives
> Thinking Ahead
> Effective Delegation
> Monitoring of Quality
> Motivation and Staff Management
> Communication
> Staff Development and Training
> Management of Outposted or Contracted out Services

Finally, in this section, it is relevant to set out the Role and Competencies of the Director of Finance, as envisaged in the NHS Executive booklet, and these are:

Main purpose

To lead and develop the finance function, so that it provides management with the advice, information and expertise to enable the provision of the best possible standards of health care.

Key accountabilities

- To define and develop the strategic vision and direction of the finance function so that it is able to set challenging objectives for the future in response to changing needs.

- To direct, lead, plan, organise and control resources in order to implement strategy and to provide monitoring and review processes to assess function effectiveness.

- To contribute to, advise on and participate in the corporate management of the Health Authority/Trust in order to provide the best possible health care within given resources.

- To promote optimum standards of professionalism within finance to ensure compliance with external standards and best practice.

- To recruit, deploy, develop, train, review and motivate staff to fulfil function objectives.

- To provide the highest possible quality of service to meet customer needs within available resources.

3

Central government funding/NHSE controls

Introduction

Regional Health Authorities receive the major part of their funds for both revenue and capital expenditure from central government via the Department of Health. Each RHA is given a capital and revenue cash limit for the provision of health services to the population living in their region. The amount of the cash limit is related to the size of the population in the area and is then allocated by the RHA between itself and the DHAs in its region.

If the RHA overspends the cash limits, this must be carried forward and deducted from the cash limit for the next year. If underspending occurs, up to 1% of the revenue cash limit and 10% of the capital cash limit can be carried forward to the next year. Any underspending greater than this is lost to the RHA. Flexibility is also possible between revenue and capital cash limits in one year up to a maximum transfer of 10% on the capital and 1% on the revenue cash limits.

RHAs may make local arrangements with individual health authorities for a limited amount of transfers between revenue and capital allocations and the carry forward of underspending on the cash limits.

Hospitals and community services which are under the control of the DHAs are required to pay capital charges to the RHA for the use of their fixed assets. This income to the RHA is then distributed to the DHAs for revenue expenditure. Income from the sale of fixed assets used by the DHAs is paid to the RHA. This is then distributed to the DHAs for capital expenditure in whatever way they think is most beneficial to the service.

Controls, by the central government directly through the Department of Health, or via the NHSE, are an important feature of the administration of the NHS. This chapter deals with the outlines of financial, audit and other controls, but other chapters of this Book also deal with the subject, particularly:

Chapter	Page(s)
4	37-43
6	60
9	81
10	Generally

National fund allocations

National allocation

The funds made available nationally to the NHS are announced in the November Budget Statement. The total planned central government expenditure on health in 1994/95 for the UK was £37.1 billion.

Government expenditure on the NHS is under two main headings, Hospitals and Community Health Services (HCHS) and Family Health Services (FHS), each of which is sub-divided into revenue and capital. Other expenditure headings are the Central Health and Miscellaneous Services (CHMS), providing services which can most effectively be administered centrally, and the administrative costs of the Department of Health.

In addition to Government funding, other sources of finance are as follows:

- Income from charges and other receipts (mainly land sales). These sources fund approximately 8% of total NHS expenditure.

- Sums of money donated by individuals or organisations to be used either at the discretion of the Authority for the welfare of patients or staff, or for a specific purpose in accordance with a bequest or trust. These non-exchequer funds are considered separately in Chapter 11.

One of the major debates surrounding HCHS finance, relates to the national revenue allocations and inflation. Depending on the inflation index used, differing conclusions can be drawn regarding the real purchasing power of Health Authorities.

In recent years, cost improvement programmes, or so called internally generated funds, also need to be considered, producing at least three commonly used measures of growth in NHS resources:

- real terms increase, using a measure of inflation in the economy as a whole;

- real terms increase, using a health service specific price index;

- both points above plus cost improvement programmes.

Each of these measures is compared with a target growth figure based on the estimated percentage real change in expenditure necessary to cope with changes in demography, advances in medicine and the funding implications of Government policies.

Cash limits

Cash limits have covered the majority of Government expenditure since 1976. Until 1981 however, expenditure plans were produced on a constant price basis, enabling the measurement of the movement in the real level of expenditure (volume). Volume planning was criticised as protecting public expenditure from inflation, and thus, in 1981, the move was made to cash planning. Plans are now expressed in cash terms based on a predicted level of inflation and these are translated directly into cash limits. Thus when inflation (pay or price increases) is above the forecast, there is no automatic assurance that the excess will be funded.

Revenue allocations to RHAs

Since the inception of the NHS four distinct periods can be identified:

- 1948-70 – allocations were based on existing services. The 1962 Hospital Plan was designed to achieve a more equal distribution of hospital beds, but generally the variations that existed before 1948 in services were perpetuated.

- 1971-76 – the 'Crossman Formula' calculated allocations based on population served, adjusted for age and sex, beds and caseload. The scale of the inter-regional differences necessitated a ten year timetable for implementation.

- 1977-89 – the Resource Allocation Working Party (RAWP) was established in 1975 with the objective of allocating Hospital and Community service resources in a way which would eventually provide equal access to health care for people in equal need. RAWP reported in 1976 and the formula was introduced in 1977. The introduction of the formula resulted in the disparities between the better provided and the less well provided parts of the country being reduced.

    Some elements of the formula received criticism however, and the NHS Management Board reviewed the operation of the formula, producing a final report in July 1988. The changes recommended in the report were never implemented and have now been superseded by the changed method of allocation following the implementation of 'Working for Patients'.

- 1990 onwards – Resident/Capitation Based Funding – A major change in resource allocation methodology commenced in 1990/91 with the move to resident population based funding.

    Each Region's population is 'weighted' to reflect the demands placed on health services by the different age groups. These 'capitation rates' are based on the estimated expenditure per head for different age groups and certain geographical supplements are then built into allocations.

Cross-boundary flows (CBFs) are not taken into account in allocations – they are now the subject of contracts. It was originally the Government's intention that full weighted capitation funding would be achieved at Regional level by 1992/93 but in allocations for 1991/92 it was announced that this process would be at a slower rate in order that all Regions receive a minimum level of growth. Subsequently, lower growth levels in the service for 1993 onwards, due to economic factors have led to a likelihood of this objective not being achieved until 1994/95 or even 1995/96.

Revenue allocations to Districts and GP Fundholders

Regions have some discretion in determining their own sub-regional allocation formula, but any mechanism must be clear, simple and stable and needs to be on 'broadly the same basis' as the national formula. In the first year (1991/92), each District's allocation reflected the actual costs of care for its own residents, (ie. by an increase to reflect the cost of outward CBFs of residents and reductions to reflect the cost of patients treated who are residents of other Districts). This placed Districts in a position to purchase broadly the services currently received by its residents, and in most parts of the country was implemented successfully.

Regions have to decide on the speed in moving Districts' allocations to the assessed weighted capitation allocation. In the longer term it is planned that capital charges will be incorporated within the general distribution of resources subject to Weighted Capitation.

FHS allocations

FHS expenditure remains largely non cash limited and at present is assumed to continue at the existing level (ie. not be subject to a weighted capitation approach). However, GP Fundholder expenditure on Practice staff/premises and GP computing are subject to cash limits which will be accounted for by RHAs although expenditure will be administered by FHSAs. These allocations to the RHA are currently ring-fenced and cannot be transferred to HCHS. FHSA administration costs are also subject to cash limits. Although indicative amounts are provided to the RHA for both primary and secondary sectors, there is no ring-fencing and funds are allocated to these sectors according to the RHAs priorities. RHAs, are now giving consideration to how, over a longer timescale, a joint Capitation approach between FHSA and HCHS expenditure could be developed to ensure the overall level of resources in each community is appropriate to its needs and as equitable as possible.

From April 1991 approved General Practices became responsible for budgets for certain non-emergency health treatment and are now acting as purchasers of services (see Chapter 2, page 16: 'General Practitioner (GP) Fundholders') Allocations have been transferred from funds available to Direct Health Authorities. Form 1993/94 onwards, the GPFH initiative was enlarged, to take a somewhat greater proportion of the Purchasing responsibility from the relevant DHA.

Capital allocations

A new definition of HCHS capital expenditure (see Chapter 7) was introduced on 1 April 1991. This reduced the threshold above which spending is classified as capital from £7,500 to £1,000. Thus more spending was to be counted as capital and £120m was transferred nationally from HCHS revenue to capital in 1991/92 to reflect this. This change was partially revised on 1 April 1993 back to £5,000, because of over complexity in the original system, with an equivalent reversal of cash limit back to revenue.

Capital expenditure by NHS Trusts is financed through accumulated depreciation, surpluses and borrowing through the External Financing Limit (EFL) mechanism (see Chapter 5). For the remainder of the NHS, a separate capital allocation continues.

This is currently allocated between regions on a RAWP based formula. Regions allocate to Districts in line with their strategic programmes. The capital allocation is split into differing programmes such as:

- major building schemes;
- medical equipment costing more than £50,000;
- ambulance services;
- priority services such as:
    - mental handicap
    - mental illness.

A proportion is delegated to Districts for items of medical equipment, vehicles, minor building alterations, fire precautions and staff housing. Medium-sized schemes may be delegated to Districts, but overall financial management is retained at Regional level. By 1995 it is likely that all or almost all Capital will go via the Trust EFL mechanism.

Joint finance

Joint financing was introduced in 1976 to promote collaboration between health and local authorities. Funds are allocated through RHAs to Districts according to the incidence of mental handicap and mental illness and the size of the over-75 population. The purpose of the fund is to 'pump prime' initiatives which will introduce new services, extend existing services, or prevent the premature abandonment of services which already exist. Funding from this source is time limited and responsibility must transfer to either Social Services, the Health Authority or a voluntary organisation.

Funding approved is normally for a period of five or seven years but can in some cases be provided for up to 10 years at 100% with a tapering effect to a maximum of 13 years in total. This latter approach has become more commonplace given its relevance to the key Care in the Community issue.

Constituent authorities – health, local, family health service authorities, voluntary bodies – prepare and approve a programme of schemes through the Joint Consultative Committee (JCC). Each scheme requires the specific approval of the sponsoring body and the health authority set out in a Memorandum of Agreement. This document explains the benefits of the scheme proposed and details the funding arrangements as the initial joint finance diminishes.

The JCC is supported by the Joint Care Planning Team (JCPT) which uses joint officer groups to develop specific policy proposals.

The direct transfer of funds was introduced through the 'Community Care' initiatives in 1983 to promote the discharge of patients from hospitals to the Community. This mechanism allows the permanent transfer of funds through savings achieved in health authority services.

Joint Finance is in facilitating the implementation of the 'Caring for People' part of the 1990 White Paper. Care in the Community which flows from this White Paper is a major issue requiring effective collaboration between Health (DHAs, FHSAs and Trusts), Local Authority Social Services Departments and GP Fundholders.

Audit arrangements

External audit

The main purpose of an external audit is to report on the published accounts of an organisation and to inform the readers whether the accounts show a true and fair review of the year's transactions and the balances at the year end. Any reservations are expressed in the form of qualified reports. While the typical commercial external audit is focused on the audit report, there is an underlying duty to consider the quality of the accounting records and fraud, if sufficiently material to affect the reader's view of the accounts. The external audit approach is generally based heavily on developing an understanding of the client, its business and systems and placing reliance on controls where they exist. Any other services which may be provided are in addition to the statutory audit role or the work needed to support the audit report.

Internal audit

The size and complexity of large organisations creates the need to review and evaluate objectively procedures and activities. This process is known as the internal audit. While this once took the form of a substitute for internal check or internal control in relation to financial transactions, modern internal audit is an operational review function which evaluates and tests managerial as well as financial control and information systems and operating efficiency.

Whereas the external auditor has a duty to report to the public, internal auditors are engaged by management and report to them. External auditors regard internal auditors, therefore, as a part of the overall structure of internal control in the organisation and may rely on their work as a part of their audit. Internal audit work, well performed may reduce the amount of external audit work required to support the audit report.

NHS audit

External audit

The scope of the external audit of public sector bodies is more extensive than that required of companies; it includes not just the 'true and fair' view but also the issues of public stewardship and accountability, ie. legality, value for money and regularity.

Within government the National Audit Office is responsible for many Appropriation Account audits including that for the NHS within the Department of Health. Responsibility for the audit of individual health authorities within the NHS, however, passed from the Department of Health to the Audit Commission on 1 October 1990 – to start with the year ending 31 March 1991. The scope of the audit has also been amended to place more emphasis on value for money issues.

The Audit Commission was established in 1982 to control the external audit of local authorities and employs the District Audit Service to undertake about 70% of its workload. The balance of the audits, are conducted by the large professional auditing firms. All work is performed according to the Audit Commission's Code of Audit Practice.

Under the Audit Commission a significant percentage of time each year will be spent on value for money topics, initially a review of the management arrangements for securing economy, efficiency and effectiveness followed by detailed studies. The material for detailed studies is all prepared by the Audit Commission in advance, based on preliminary investigations and pilot studies from which detailed briefing reports are prepared for the auditors who are also trained in their use.

The external auditors are also required by the Code of Audit Practice to issue to the Authority a management letter setting the agenda for a discussion of major issues and to the Director of Finance an internal control letter setting out the detailed control weaknesses discovered during the audit.

The external auditor may also issue a report 'in the public interest' directly to the Secretary of State in exceptional circumstances.

Internal audit

During the 1980s internal audit in the NHS was developed from the 'weak and ineffective' service cited in the 1981 Public Accounts Committee report on internal audit in the Public Sector to a much more robust service today based on the NHS Internal Audit Standards (1990) and the NHS Internal Audit Manual (1987).

The Standards are primarily a qualitative statement and reflect best professional auditing practice. They set the framework within which the Manual provides guidance as to the conduct of work and the principal issues of concern in the NHS.

The Manual is continually under review to ensure that it reflects current issues. The internal audit required to be maintained by a Health Authority or Trust, must be capable of meeting minimum standards as set out in the Manual.

Value for money initiatives

Value for money (VFM) initiatives in the NHS have included:

- cost improvement programmes run by individual health authorities to generate savings and improve efficiency;

- an initiative encouraging health authorities to generate additional income by their own activities. Launched in early 1988, this is now supported by legislative changes which clarify and extend authorities' ability to act in a more commercial and entrepreneurial manner, while maintaining safeguards in relation to patient care;

- the Department of Health published the booklet *Comparing Health Authorities* in early 1988 which examines trends over time of selected indicators. These indicators show improvements in the national figures for the efficient use of beds and cost per acute case. The indicators also suggest that there are significant variations between districts in service provision and efficiency;

- the NHS Executive has initiated a number of national studies and established a small central VFM unit. The initial work of the unit has been to develop a computerised database for VFM initiatives and good practice and this is now available to health authorities;

- CIPFA and HFMA (the Healthcare Financial Management Association) have jointly published many booklets on NHS Finance including a *Health service VFM guide*;

- the National Audit Office published *Value For Money Developments in the NHS* in 1986.

    This report found that the target value of cost improvements contained in the individual programmes submitted by different authorities varied significantly, both as between districts and as between regions.

The internal market in the NHS, with its split of purchaser and provider, automatically provides built in value for money incentives especially in a cash limited environment. The Audit Commission is to progress (as with local government), the publication of performance 'league tables' of NHS Trusts and Authorities and the first of these appeared in the summer of 1994.

The NHS Task Force on Corporate Governance (see following section) has recommended the formal establishment of an Audit Committee for NHS Boards to oversee effective internal financial controls and liaison with the external auditor.

Corporate Governance in the NHS

The Cadbury report on Corporate Governance, was published in late 1992 and was the result of a Committee of Inquiry chaired by Sir Adrian Cadbury. The committee was established to ask some searching questions about the way companies are run and the relationships between shareholders, directors and auditors.

The report recommended a Code of Conduct for the way in which companies are run, setting out specific roles for the Chairman, Chief Executive, and the public responsibility of auditors.

The NHSE has been very active in pursuing the principles of Corporate Governance and their application to the health service. A Corporate Governance Task Force has recently reported to the NHSE Chief Executive and its central recommendations are:

- there should be an NHS code of conduct;

- a code of accountability for NHS boards should be adopted as the basis of the delegation of functions from Secretary of State to NHS authorities and trusts;

- directors of NHS boards should declare private interests which are material and relevant to NHS business and these should be recorded in board minutes: directorships should be published in the annual report (see below);

- clearer definitions of the functions of chairmen and non-executive directors should be introduced and form the basis of the appointment and induction processes;

- improved arrangements for the formal induction and development of newly appointed chairmen and non-executive directors should be introduced as soon as possible;

- the NHS Management Executive should clarify the position on all financial constraints which apply to NHS authorities and trusts and should communicate them to the Service in one clear and readily-understood summary;

- the current Directions on Financial Management should be urgently updated to take account of developments since they were last issued in 1991;

- NHS boards should be required to establish formal committees on Audit and on Remuneration and Terms of Service of Executive Directors;

- NHS boards should be reminded of their responsibility for high standards of financial stewardship through effective financial planning and strategic financial control and through maximising value for money, and should receive guidance on:

    - organising and presenting financial and performance information to NHS boards;
    - audit and remuneration committees;
    - financial control; and
    - finance training for board-level non-specialists;

- standing orders of NHS boards should prescribe the terms on which committees and sub-committees may be delegated functions and should include, where adopted, the schedule of decisions reserved to the board;

- NHS authorities should be obliged to publish an annual report (already mandatory for trusts) on their performance in purchasing health service and on their stewardship of public finances; and

- the total emoluments from NHS sources of chairmen, executive directors and non-executive directors should be published in annual reports.

4

The NHS Accounting Environment

Introduction and overview

Substantial changes to the financial and organisational framework of the NHS were made in the *NHS and Community Care Act 1990* and were operational from 1 April 1991.

The key changes which affected finance managers include:

- the separation of responsibility for purchasing and providing services, with the primary responsibility of district health authorities (DHAs) being to assess health needs and purchase health care for their residents;

- a change in funding arrangements to resident based funding for DHAs from 1 April 1991 and then to weighted capitation; DHA allocations cover their residents. The home district of a patient is expected to pay for the health care provided either within agreed contracts or under extra-contractual referral arrangements. However, if a patient is registered with a General Practitioner who is a fundholder (GPFH), the fundholder will be expected to pay for some types of health care (see page 16);

- the opportunity for providers of health care services to become NHS Trusts;

- the majority of income for provider units will be obtained through a system of contracting. Where contracts are not in place, invoices will be issued to the patient's district of residence or relevant GPFH to recover the cost of treatment;

- expenditure of DHAs as purchasers of health care will be identified separately from that of directly managed provider units (DMUs) and common services;

- costing, pricing and invoicing will be devolved closer to the point of delivery of services;

- the cost of using capital assets will be charged to units of management and common services.

Financial environment

For the finance function, these changes represent a significant increase in the complexity of the financial environment. They also introduced elements of risk through uncertainty in the flows of income. In future, in their PURCHASER role, DHAs will need to:

- provide funds for their DMUs to meet the costs of treating their residents, whether under contracts or as extra-contractual referrals;

- make payments within cash limits for both contracted services and extra-contractual referrals to providers outside the district, including NHS Trusts and other districts' DMUs.

PROVIDER units need to:

- have sufficient income from contracts and extra-contractual referrals to meet their operating expenditure;

- have arrangements in place to invoice purchasers for the treatment of their patients;

- ensure income is collected.

In their management role for DMUs, DHAs need to ensure that DMUs have these arrangements in place.

Monitoring and control

Maintaining financial viability within DHAs will require changes to monitoring and control mechanisms. In addition, the format of the annual accounts has been revised. The revised form reflects both purchaser and provider activities and incorporates commercial accounting standards (adapted to reflect differences in the public sector). Annual Accounts are dealt with in Chapter 10.

Monitoring and control systems and procedures within a DHA need to be reviewed. Information produced for monitoring and control should be sufficient for local management needs and to satisfy the reporting requirements of Regional Health Authorities (RHAs) and the NHS Management Executive.

The District Director of Finance will be responsible for ensuring that financial systems and procedures are established which can maintain control and ensure that financial duties are met. The most significant of these is managing within the cash limit.

Accounting framework

The new financial environment requires the development of an accounting framework which covers a substantial proportion of the financial control and accountability issues facing DHAs. These include:

1. funding flows;
2. cash management;
3. financial accounts
4. financial control.

If the Director of Finance does not implement systems and procedures covering the above, the likely risks will be:

- loss of financial control;
- qualified accounts;
- failure to meet financial duties, including keeping within the cash limit.

In most DHAs, the lynchpin in establishing and maintaining systems and procedures will usually be the Financial Controller acting under delegated authority from the Director of Finance. The organisational arrangements in each authority, in particular with respect to the level of devolution to provider units, will determine responsibility and authority.

The Accounting Framework

> These changes were reflected, in detail, in the NHS Executive's Financial Management Training Initiative publication 'The Accounting Framework' which was issued in 1991, and is revised annually in detail. The Framework is based on four modules, each covering the four main aspects of financial control and accountability mentioned on page 35: '*Introduction and overview*' and also contains a practical example of the components of the accounting framework, based on a hypothetical health authority and containing the requisite journal entries and ledger accounts.
>
> This publication is one of the two main volumes issued by the NHSE that will be of great practical value to students. The other document 'Health Authority Manual for Accounts' is covered in Chapter 10, and study of both publications is important. There are other, very detailed, NHSE books, including a separate manual for NHS Trusts.

The following paragraphs pick out some of the more relevant (to students, as opposed to practitioners) sections of 'The Accounting Framework' publication, which is based upon a District Health Authority.

Funding flows

Principles

(a) At Regional level:

- Regional Health Authorities will continue to receive funding allocations from the Department of Health;
- this funding will be supplemented by capital charges payments made by DMUs within the Region;
- the Region will allocate its money between:
    - RHA administration;
    - Family Health Services;
    - purchaser allocations to DHAs and GP fundholders;
    - costs of contracts between the RHA and provider units

- the RHA may provide common services (eg. ambulance services, supplies, computing services) which are recharged to DHAs and other users.

(b) At District level:

- DHAs' main source of funding will be their allocations from their RHAs;

- the level of funding for 1991/92 will be sufficient for a DHA to purchase broadly the current level of services for its residents wherever these are provided;

- DHA allocations will be reduced where GPFHs have patients resident in the district. These funds will be used for budgets for GPFHs;

- capital charges are payable to the RHA by DHAs in respect of the assets used by their DMUs and common services;

- income will be received for services provided to residents of other DHAs and to patients of GPFHs;

- payments will be made to other providers for services provided to district residents;

- a major source of expenditure will continue to be the operating expenditure of the DHA where there are DMUs.

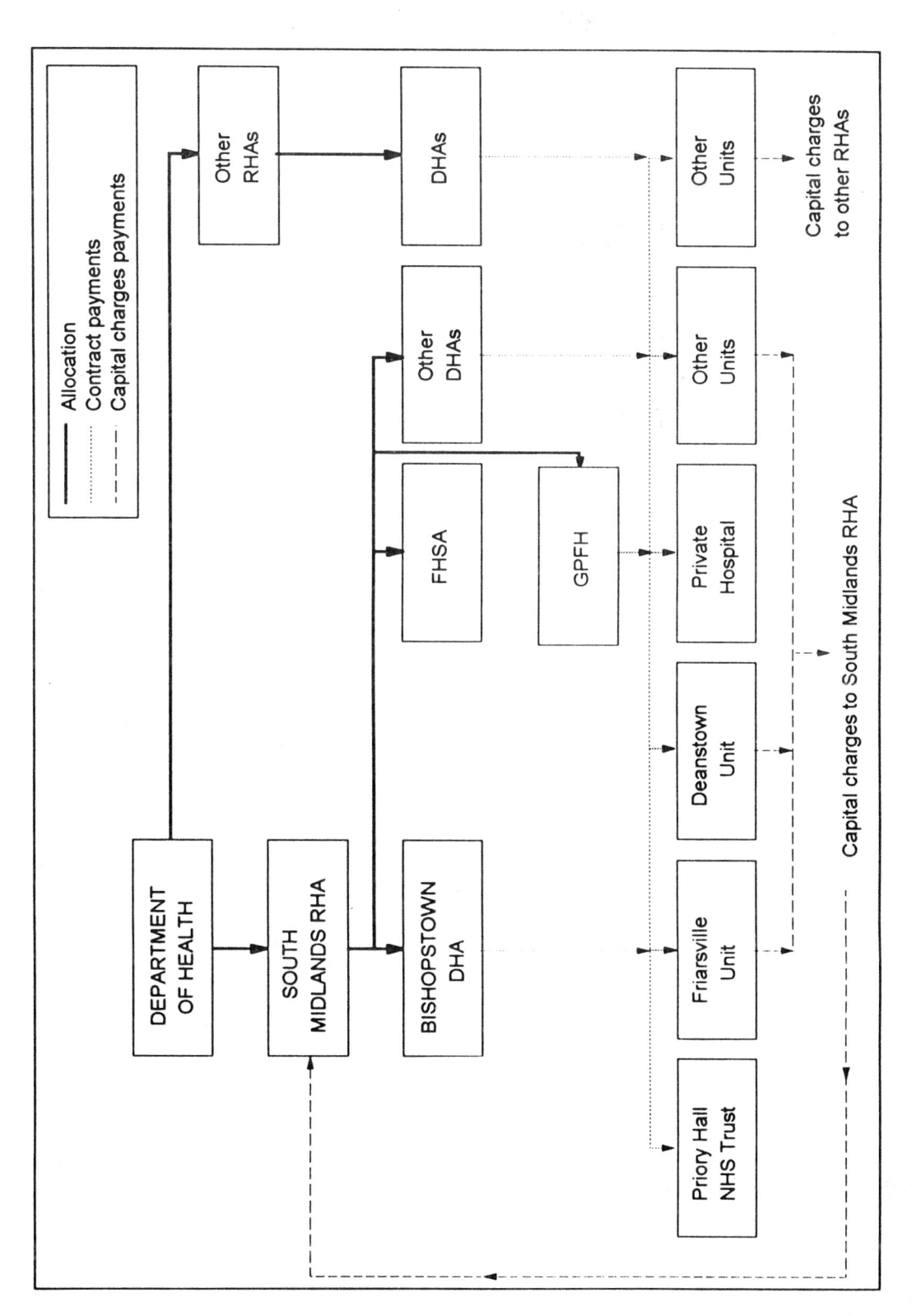

A table of funding flows from 'The Accounting Framework'

Cash management

(a) DHAs

Cash management is the process of ensuring that sufficient cash is available on a daily basis to meet commitments and that the Authority operates within its cash limit. Funding for the payment of staff and for goods and services is obtained from the Department of Health by requisition into the Health Authority's Bank Account or transfer by Paymaster General's Order. Each Authority is requires to establish a PGO account which enables payment to be made between Authorities without cash being drawn from the Exchequer. Cash requirements are forecast to the Department of Health through a series of weekly and monthly returns (the FIS returns).

The three main areas of 'risk' in relation to cash flows are:

- extra-contractual referrals payable to external providers by the purchaser;

- extra-contractual referrals chargeable to other purchasers for services provided by DMUs;

- potential timing mismatch between income received through DMU activities (eg. through late payment) and the need to meet purchaser commitments on a scheduled and timely basis;

Cash management is the process whereby:

- the impact of the change on cash flow is established;

- a strategy is developed to manage the risk;

- cash flow performance is monitored and projections updated;

- corrective action is taken when performance differs from plans.

(b) NHS Trusts

NHS Trusts must ensure that they have sufficient cash available on a daily basis to meet their commitments. Cash is generated from contracts with and extra contractual referrals from purchasers as well as private patient income and other income generation initiatives.

To assist in cash management, NHS Trusts are permitted to invest surplus cash and are allowed to borrow money within annually agreed limits. This is further discussed in Chapter 5.

The cash management chapter of 'The Accounting Framework' summary gives the following guidance for a District Health Authority:

Key elements

Outflows:

- operating costs of DMUs and the common services function;
- expenditure of the purchasing function and DHA administration;
- contract payments for the purchasing function;
- payment of invoices for extra-contractual referrals.

Inflows:

- cash drawn under revenue allocation for purchasing;
- receipt of contract income from other purchasers;
- receipt of extra-contractual referral income from other purchasers.

Administrative issues

Successful cash flow management requires appropriate administrative support including:

- appropriate information systems and procedures to link patients to contracts and interface with the invoicing system;
- effective debtor management and cash collection, including resolution of queries with purchasers;
- appropriate information systems and procedures for the identification of extra-contractual referral commitments and the verification and authorisation of payments by the purchasing function, including resolution of queries within providers;
- good liaison within the unit or purchasing function for the resolution of queries;
- banking arrangements in place and staff clear on the working arrangements for each account.

Monitoring systems

Systems need to be in place to ensure that the original cash forecasts are regularly monitored and updated so that corrective action can be taken.

Financial viability

If income and expenditure plans are not achieved, additional pressures will be placed on cash management which may result in the DHA not staying within its cash limit.

Financial accounts

This Chapter is concerned with the new format of annual financial accounts and returns for the year ending 31 March 1992 and subsequent years. Details of these arrangements are contained in Chapter 10 of this Book.

Financial controls

The NHS reforms continue to place the responsibility for the overall financial performance of a health authority on the DHA. The Director of Finance is responsible for ensuring that adequate systems of financial control are in place. The one change to this accountability is where an NHS Trust has been formed within the District. Responsibility for the financial performance of the Trust rests with the Trust's Board and Director of Finance.

The role of the Director of Finance encompasses not only the establishment and maintenance of financial control systems and procedures but also reporting to the Health Authority on breaches of financial controls, including failure of the DMUs common services or purchasing function to attain financial viability. The overall framework for financial control is as follows:

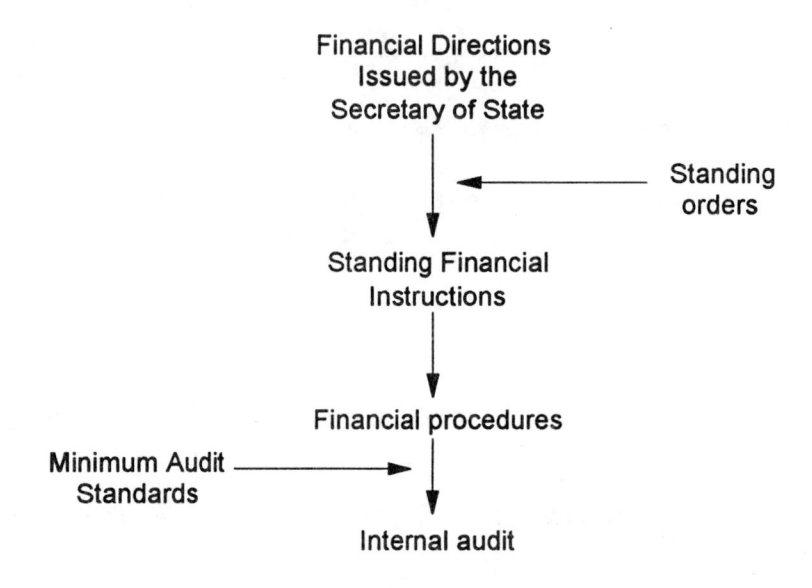

```
              Financial Directions
                  Issued by the
                Secretary of State
                        |
                        | ←──────── Standing orders
                        ↓
              Standing Financial
                  Instructions
                        |
                        ↓
              Financial procedures
   Minimum Audit ──────→|
     Standards          ↓
                  Internal audit
```

Source: The Accounting Framework, DoH, 1991

All health authorities continue to be required to maintain sound financial management of all their activities and services, including the purchasing function, DMUs and common services.

In summary, health authorities (including both executive and non-executive members) are required to:

- approve annual financial budgets;

- monitor actual financial performance against those budgets;

- lay down financial controls to safeguard the authority's resources;

- ensure that the cash limit for the financial year is kept.

Each health authority will determine the financial responsibilities of individual executive members and health authority officers. The General Manager (who is an executive member of the authority) has overall executive responsibility for all the authority's activities, is responsible to the authority for ensuring the authority remains within its cash limit and must ensure the authority is provided with financial information. The Director of Finance (who is also an executive member of the authority) will provide this information and financial advice to the authority and is responsible for designing, implementing and supervising the financial control and accounting systems.

DHAs need to be satisfied in particular with the financial procedures relating to DMUs. These procedures will specify the limits to delegated financial authority, including limits for the authorisation of contracts.

There are a number of different elements contributing to the framework for financial control. These include:

- financial directions;
- standing orders;
- standing financial instructions;
- financial control procedures;
- internal audit.

Each of these elements are now briefly explained:

Financial directions

Financial directions are issued by the Secretary of State for Health and set down in broad terms, the responsibilities and requirements for financial control in health authorities. These are minimum statutory requirements and should be the basis upon which authorities develop their own financial control policies, including standing financial instructions.

Standing orders

Standing orders are drawn up by the health authority and regulate the authority's business and its meetings. They normally include reference to the control of the authority's tendering and contracting procedures. They may also refer to the authority's standing financial instructions.

Standing financial instructions

Standing financial instructions (SFIs) are drawn up by the health authority and describe in detail the way in which the financial directions are put into practice in the authority. The SFIs must be adopted by the health authority, subsequent to which the Director of Finance is delegated the task of drawing up and implementing detailed financial control procedures. Model SFIs are being produced by the Healthcare Financial Management Association (HFMA), on behalf of the NHS Management Executive, as a guide to health authorities.

Financial control procedures

Financial control procedures describe the operation of each financial system, clearly identifying procedures, checks, controls, responsibilities and limits to authority. Procedures should be fully documented and relevant staff trained to follow them.

Internal audit

Internal audit is required to be maintained by a health authority, meeting the mandatory standards as set out in the NHS Internal Audit Manual. The primary role of internal audit is to review, appraise and report to management on the soundness, adequacy and application of financial management controls, and the extent of compliance with established policies, plans and procedures. (Audit matters are further considered in Chapter 3, page 29: '*Audit Arrangements*'.)

Standing orders and standing financial Instructions will be well known to finance staff in local government, where they perform similar functions. A typical index to a set of standing orders produced by a Health Authority, includes:

- Meetings
- Committees and sub-committees
- Custody of seal and sealing of documents
- Officers – appointment and declaration of interest
- Tendering and contract procedures
- Healthcare contracts

and the whole set is 24 pages long.

The Draft Model Standing Financial Instructions referred to above, contains the following entries in its index:

Foreword
Introduction

Section	Contents
A Core	Business planning
	Budgetary control
	Annual accounts
	Bank and PGO accounts
	Payment of staff
	Non-pay expenditure
	Income and cash handling
	Internal audit
	Financial Reports to the Board
	Losses, disposals and condemnations
B Trust	External borrowing
	Contracting
	Investments
	Charitable funds
	Security of assets
	Private finance
	Patients property
	Stores
C Health authorities	Purchasing and contracting
	Cash limit
	Trading undertakings
D Family health service authorities	Payment to independent contractors
	GP fundholders
E Intermediate tier	Allocations
	Monitoring of authorities
	Education and training contracts
	GP fundholders

The Foreword indicates that SFIs are policy statements which are not meant to provide detailed advice: they are therefore to be read in conjunction with the detailed departmental and financial procedure notes of individual health bodies. The SFIs are mandatory and apply to all staff working for the HA/Trust or a constituent organisation.

National Health Service Trusts

Introduction

NHS Trusts are hospitals and other units which have their own Boards of Directors. The Board consists of a non-executive Chairman (appointed by the Secretary of State), up to five non-executive directors (of which two are appointed by the RHA) and an equal number of executive directors, up to a maximum of five (including the Chief Executive and Director of Finance). In contrast to DMU's, they are operationally independent of District Health Authorities and they have the freedom to:

- acquire, own and dispose of assets to ensure the most effective use is made of them;

- make cases for capital developments direct to the NHS Management Executive;

- borrow money, within annually agreed limits, primarily for new building and equipment and for upgrading existing buildings;

- create management structures;

- employ staff, determine staffing structures, and set terms and conditions of employment;

- advertise their services, within the guidelines set down by professional codes of practice on such advertising.

Trusts are accountable to the Secretary of State (via the NHSE).

In several significant respects, the financial regime of NHS Trusts differs from that of DMUs. These differences are covered in this Chapter.

In particular:

- trusts receive no direct funding from the Department and must earn all their income;

- trusts can borrow funds, within annually approved limits, for purposes such as acquiring or replacing assets;

- trusts usually retain depreciation and any surpluses after meeting financial obligations and can use this money to repay loans, to invest or for capital spending;

- trusts must make a 6% return on their assets and break even taking one year with another;

- trust accounts are commercial in style, following Companies Acts requirements where appropriate.

As with DHAs, trusts must ensure that they have sufficient cash available on a daily basis to meet their commitments. See Chapter 4, page 37: *'The Accounting Framework'* for further detail on Cash Management.

Revenue and pricing

Like other health service units, Trusts earn most of their revenue from contracts to provide health services. These contracts are made with health authorities, GP fundholders and private patients or their insurance companies.

Trusts may also receive funds:

- from extra-contractual referrals;

- for supporting medical and dental education and research;

- for the education and training of other health care professionals;

- from income generating activities.

Trusts price their services on the basis of covering their costs, including depreciation on their assets, and achieving a 6% rate of return on the current value of their net assets.

Trusts are expected to attribute their costs using principles common to the NHS as a whole. They are not allowed to plan to cross-subsidise services between contracts and are expected to use marginal costing only when they have unplanned spare capacity arising during the year.

When setting prices for NHS contracts, Trusts should not plan to achieve more than a 6% rate of return on their assets, since higher rates would reduce the volume of patient care which health authorities could afford to purchase. Contracts with the private sector are not subject to this restriction and these contracts should be priced at the level the market will bear, subject to the need to make a minimum of 6% return on assets. If a higher return than 6% is made this may be used to reduce the prices which would otherwise be charged to NHS purchasers.

Originating capital debt

Each Trust owns its assets – land, buildings, and equipment. The value of the net assets (assets less liabilities) transferred to a Trust when it is set up (except any assets donated to the NHS since 1948) is matched by an originating capital debt which is owed by the Trust to the Consolidated Fund.

The originating capital debt is made up of two elements:

- interest bearing debt (IBD) which has defined interest and repayment terms; and

- public dividend capital (PDC) which is a form of long term Government finance on which the Trust pays dividends to the Government.

The balance between IBD and PDC is set individually for each Trust by the Secretary of State, with the consent of the Treasury.

Asset valuation

Trust assets are valued on the same basis as those of the directly managed sector. Generally:

- Land and buildings held for operational use are valued by the District Valuer at their open market value for existing use. If land and buildings become surplus to requirements they are valued at open market value for alternative use.

- Other tangible fixed assets, eg. medical equipment or furniture, are valued at their current cost.

Intangible assets, such as intellectual property, are valued individually.

Current assets, for instance stocks and debtors, are valued in accordance with normal accountancy principles.

All Trusts need to maintain asset registers to record and value fixed assets, which should include any donated assets.

Borrowing and debt repayment

There are two sources of finance to enable a Trust to maintain and expand its facilities and to obtain working capital:

- funds generated by the Trust itself from depreciation and retained surpluses, or from sales of land, buildings and equipment;

- external borrowing from either the Secretary of State or the private sector.

Trusts are able to borrow from the Secretary of State or commercial sources. The Secretary of State can guarantee a Trust's loan from the private sector which would reduce borrowing costs. In seeking such a guarantee the Trust would have to demonstrate distinct advantages over borrowing from the Secretary of State.

A Trust needs to demonstrate its ability to pay interest on, and repay, loans before they are made. Trusts may not borrow money before they need it. It is unacceptable for them to borrow at low rates from the Government and put the money on deposit at a higher rate to generate income. However, Trusts are free to use interest-earning bank accounts for day-to-day transactions.

There are two sources for short term borrowing for periods up to a year:

- conventional bank overdrafts, which are most often suitable where they are likely to be significant fluctuations in the timing or amount of borrowing needed; and

- temporary borrowing from the Secretary of State to meet more significant and defined short term needs.

Borrowing is normally in the form of interest bearing loans at either fixed or variable interest rates depending on the Trust's financial position. An element of PDC finance may be considered in particular circumstances, for example where expenditure is spread over a period of years and where a building or other facility does not become operational immediately, and in the light of the Trust's overall financial position as shown in its annual business plan.

Each Trust has to repay its interest bearing debt, including the interest bearing portion of its originating capital debt, over a defined period which is related to the lives of its assets but in general does not exceed twenty years. The repayment methods are:

- equal instalments of principal;
- equal repayments;
- maturity loans, with interest rolled up during the life of the loan.

The Trust may apply to repay any interest bearing debt early, including any originating capital debt.

Business planning process

Each Trust is required to prepare an annual business plan covering three forward years. The business planning cycle for Trusts needs to align with that of health authorities because of the inter-relationship between Trust finance and service strategies and those of purchasing authorities.

Each Trust is expected to send its business plan to the NHSE by early March each year, ie. at broadly the same time as regional health authority short term plans are submitted to the NHSE. The first year of the accompanying financial proforma forms the basis for the in-year financial monitoring of the Trust.

In preparing plans Trusts need:

- to develop considered and explicit assumptions of the level of revenue purchasing power of their major purchasers over the period of the plan;
- to make clear assumptions about the likely impact of inflation over the period of the plan;
- to set out clear and well justified plans for capital developments and the funding arrangements for such developments;
- to provide sensitivity analyses based on different assumptions.

In addition, trusts need to ensure that their business planning enables them to satisfy a range of financial criteria, including, achievement of financial targets and duties, satisfactory appraisal of capital investment proposals, and consistency with the Trust's own strategy.

External Financing Limits

An External Financing Limit (EFL) is, in effect, a cash limit on net external financing for a Trust. External finance is the difference between agreed capital spending by a Trust and internally generated resources. Put simply, an EFL comprises:

- new loans taken out by the Trusts; less

- repayments of loans during the year; plus or minus

- net changes in deposits and other holdings of liquid assets.

A national total for Trust EFLs is determined through the annual PES process. The NHSE sets an individual EFL for each Trust within the national total, taking account of its business plan. A Trust can be given an EFL which is positive, zero, or negative, and is expected to keep within its EFL each year, although there is limited flexibility.

Financial duties

Each Trust has two financial duties in addition to staying within its EFL:

- to achieve its financial target. This is a real pre-interest return of 6% on the value of net assets – essentially an average of the opening and closing assets shown in the accounts;

- to break even on income and expenditure account, after payment of interest and PDC dividends, taking one year with another.

There is also a general requirement for Trusts to ensure that their activities are carried out in such a way as to achieve best value for money.

Surpluses

While Trusts have a duty at least to break even they are expected to make a revenue surplus after allowing for interest payments and dividends on PDC. Any net surplus can be used for capital expenditure, to repay loans, or for investment. Temporary cash surpluses can be held in Government Securities or in other approved public or private sector investments.

Where a Trust has a cash surplus considerably greater than its reasonable need for funds – for instance, from the sale of land or buildings at a price reflecting development gain – the Secretary of State may require the Trust to pay the Government all or part of its reserves.

Annual accounts

A Trust's annual accounts will be presented as an integrated document comprising three statements (income and expenditure account, balance sheet and cash flow statement) supported by three sections, accounting policies, notes to the income and expenditure account and notes to the balance sheet.

The annual accounts must be approved by the Trust prior to presentation at a public meeting. In normal circumstances the deadline for such a meeting should be the end of September following the end of the relevant financial year.

Accounts

Each Trust must keep proper accounts and present them annually in a specified format. The format of the accounts is based on the requirements of the Companies Acts, but with variations to reflect the special circumstances of Trusts. The accounts must show 'a true and fair view' of the Trust's financial affairs and, generally speaking, the relevant Statements of Standard Accounting Practice are followed.

The accounts are submitted to the Secretary of State and are the corporate responsibility of the Trust Board. However, the Trust's chief executive, advised by the director of finance, is responsible for ensuring, on behalf of the Board, that all accounting and financing matters are in order. This includes ensuring that:

- all public funds are properly managed and safeguarded;
- standing financial instructions are complied with; and
- the accounts of the Trust are properly presented.

The director of finance is responsible for ensuring that financial systems and controls meet the requirements of good financial management. The chief executive, advised by the director of finance, is responsible for answering, on behalf of the Trust Board, any questions on the accounts of an individual Trust, and for informing the NHSE if, at any time, the long term financial viability of the Trust is at risk.

The accounts of each Trust are audited by the Audit Commission. The National Audit Office (NAO) is responsible for auditing the consolidated accounts of NHS Trusts and laying them before Parliament. The NAO has right of access to papers and other records relating to each Trust's financial, accounting and auditing matters. Both the Audit Commission and NAO may conduct value for money studies in Trusts.

Copies of the annual accounts statements now follow:

Income and expenditure account for the year ended 31 March 19XX

	Note	£'000	(Previous year) 19XX-XX £'000
Income from activities			
Other operating income		X	X
Operating expenses		X	X
Operating surplus (Deficit)		X	X
Interest receivable		X	X
Interest payable		X	X
Surplus (Deficit) on ordinary activities		X	X
Extraordinary items		X	X
Surplus (Deficit) for the financial year		X	X
PDC Dividend payable		X	X
Retained surplus (Deficit) for the year		X	X
Surplus (deficit) brought forward		X	X
Surplus (deficit) carried forward		X	X
Financial target performance: X.X%		X.X%	X..X%

Balance sheet as at 31 March 19XX

	Note	£'000	£'000	(Previous year) 19XX-XX £'000
Fixed assets				
Intangible assets		X	X	
Tangible assets		X	X	
Current assets				
Stocks and work in progress		X	X	
Debtors		X	X	
Short-term investments		X	X	
Cash at bank and in hand		X	X	
Creditors: Amounts falling due within one year		X	X	
Net current assets (liabilities)		X	X	
Total assets less current liabilities		X	X	
Creditors: Amounts falling due after more than one year		X	X	
Financed by:				
Capital and reserves				
Public dividend capital		X	X	
Long-term loans		X	X	
Revaluation reserve		X	X	
Donation reserve		X	X	
Other reserves		X	X	
Income and expenditure account		X	X	
		X	X	

[Handwritten note next to Public dividend capital / Long-term loans: "why have both?"]

Signed on behalf of the board on (day, month, year)

Chairman

Chief executive

Cash flow Statement for the year ended 31 March 19XX

	£'000	£'000	(Previous year) £'000
Operating activities			
Cash received from customers	X		X
Cash payments to suppliers	(X)		(X)
Cash paid to and on behalf of employees	(X)		(X)
Other cash payments	(X)		(X)
Net cash inflow from operating activities		X	X
Returns on investments and servicing of finance			
Interest received		X	X
Interest paid	(X)		(X)
Interest element of finance lease rental payments	(X)		(X)
Dividends paid	(X)		(X)
Net cash outflow from returns on investments and servicing of finance		(X)	X
Investing activities			
Payments to acquire fixed assets	(X)		(X)
Receipts from sale of fixed assets	X		X
Net cash outflow from investing activities		(X)	(X)
Net cash outflow before financing		(X)	(X)
Financing			
New public dividend capital received	X		X
New long-term loans	X		X
New short-term loans	X		X
Repayment of amounts borrowed	(X)		(X)
Capital element of finance lease rental payments	(X)		(X)
Net cash inflow from financing		X	X
Increase in cash and cash equivalents		X	X

Notes to the cash flow statement

1. Reconciliation of operating surplus to net cash inflow from operating activities

	£'000	(Previous year) £'000
Operating surplus	X	X
Depreciation charges	X	X
Profit/(loss) on disposals of fixed assets	(X)	(X)
Increase in stocks	(X)	(X)
Increase in debtors	(X)	(X)
Increase in creditors	X	X
Net cash inflow from operating activities	X	X

2. Analysis of changes in cash and cash equivalents during the year

	£'000
Balance at 1 April 19XX	X
Net cash inflow	X
Balance at 31 March 19XX	X

3. Analysis of the balance of cash and cash equivalents as shown in the balance sheet

	19XX £'000	19XX £'000	Change in year £'000
Cash at bank and in hand	X	X	X
Short-term investments	X	X	X
Bank overdrafts	(X)	(X)	(X)
	X	X	X

4. Analysis of changes in financing during the year

	Public dividend capital £'000	Long-term loans £'000	Other loans £'000
Balance at 1 April 19XX	X	X	X
Cash inflow/(outflow) from financing	X	(X)	X
Balance at 31 March 19XX	X	X	X

6

Financial and business planning

National planning framework

Financial planning is an essential and integral part of NHS finance and forms a major part of the annual planning process.

The Financial Planning System (FPS) is based on a set of proformas setting out the minimum information required by the NHS Executive.

The proformas are completed by DMUs, DHAs and RHAs, each level assessing and summarising plans before onward submission. FHSAs return their plans direct to RHAs and NHS Trusts direct to NHSE Outposts. An overview of the FPS is shown below:

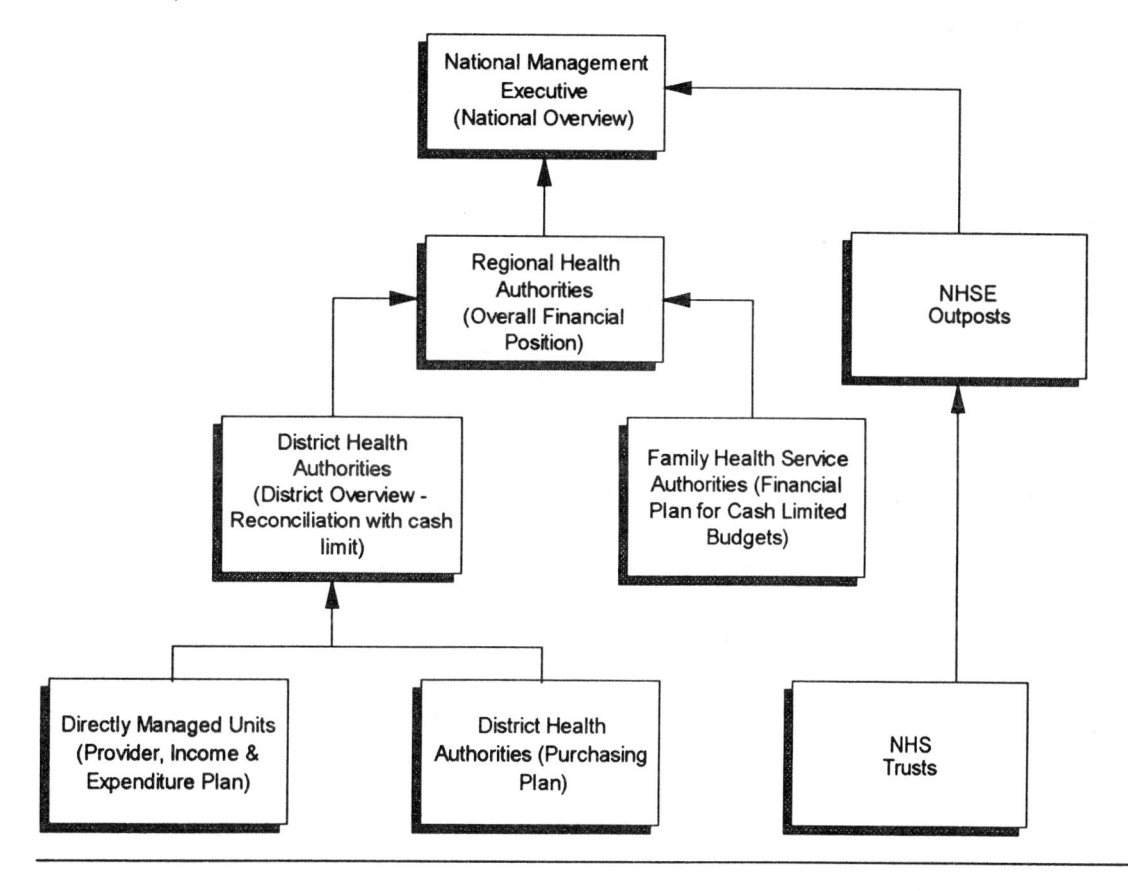

```
                    ┌─────────────────────┐
                    │ National Management │
                    │      Executive      │
                    │  (National Overview)│
                    └──────────▲──────────┘
                               │
          ┌────────────────────┴──────────┐
          │                               │
┌─────────┴──────────┐            ┌───────┴──────┐
│  Regional Health   │            │    NHSE      │
│    Authorities     │◄───────────│   Outposts   │
│ (Overall Financial │            │              │
│     Position)      │            └───────▲──────┘
└──┬──────────────┬──┘                    │
   │              │                       │
┌──┴──────────┐  ┌┴──────────────────┐    │
│District Health│ │Family Health Service│  │
│ Authorities  │ │Authorities (Financial│  │
│(District Overview│ │Plan for Cash Limited│ │
│-Reconciliation│ │    Budgets)       │    │
│with cash limit)│└───────────────────┘    │
└──▲───────────┘                           │
   │                                       │
┌──┴─────────────┬──────────────┐  ┌───────┴──┐
│Directly Managed│ │District Health│ │   NHS    │
│Units (Provider,│ │Authorities    │ │  Trusts  │
│Income &        │ │(Purchasing    │ │          │
│Expenditure Plan)│ │    Plan)     │ └──────────┘
└────────────────┘ └───────────────┘
```

57

The role of regional health authorities

RHAs will give guidance on the likely resource assumptions to be used including advice on inflation. In addition, RHAs will prepare plans for their own activities, assess and compare individual DHA and FHSA plans, and prepare a consolidated Regional plan for submission to the NHSE.

In assessing DHA and FHSA plans, the Region will be looking to ensure that plans have been prepared within the framework set, contain realistic forecasts of income and expenditure, demonstrate efficiency gains, and are within available resources.

At the end of the process of preparing and assessing plans, the RHA prepares a consolidated plan comprising:

- a summary of directly managed provider units;
- a summary of purchasing activities;
- a reconciliation of purchaser and provider plans;
- a summary of other activities;
- the requirements of FHSAs;
- the overall regional financial position.

The Regional consolidated plan is submitted to the NHSE and this forms the basis for monitoring progress during the year and also for comparison with the outturn after the year end. RHAs monitor DHAs and FHSAs.

Directly managed units

Careful business planning is essential for DMUs to ensure sufficient income is attracted, through the provision of services, to meet the total cost of the provider unit.

In compiling business plans DMUs will have regard to inflation, levels of activity and the requirement to balance expenditure to income.

Business plans should aim to minimise risk associated with income not secured by contracts and this will require working closely with purchasers in developing service contracts. Income from contracts with purchasing DHAs will be a major source of revenue for DMUs.

Other income will include that from GP fundholders, and non-NHS purchasers, which will require careful assessment and agreement where possible.

DMUs submit their income and expenditure plans together with an analysis of the sources of expected income to their managing DHA for assessment and consolidation into the overall District Financial plan, before that is submitted to the Regional Health Authority.

District health authorities

DHAs have a responsibility both as purchasing authorities in their own right and also as managers of provider units (DMUs). Districts have four key roles in the financial planning process:

- the preparation of purchasing plans;
- assessing plans of provider units and balancing those with their own purchasing plans;
- preparation of plans for other DHA activities including administration;
- compiling a picture of the overall financial position of the District.

In preparing their own plans, DHAs will have regard to the overall availability of resources, and where demand exceeds resource availability, balancing measures will need to be taken.

Purchasing plans will need to be discussed with provider units before they are finalised.

DHAs are expected to demonstrate achievement of efficiency gains in their purchasing role, by comparing changes in activity with changes in real terms expenditure.

In assessing and agreeing the plans of their directly managed provider units, DHAs will carry out a number of steps including:

- checking that commitments have been provided for;
- analysing the risk from non-contracted income expectations;
- checking the adequacy of contingency plans;
- looking for efficiency gains;
- assessing the overall plan for realism.

Family Health Service Authorities

FHAs will prepare plans for submission to RHAs, the main elements being:

- to manage within cash allocations;
- to avoid overcommitting recurrent resources;
- to manage in-year cost pressure within recurrent resources.

Financial processes will need to be in place to ensure that the plans contain balanced and realistically forecast income and expenditure.

Plans are submitted to the RHA for inclusion in the consolidated Regional plan.

NHS Trust business plans

Each Trust is required to prepare an annual business plan covering a three year period. The business planning cycle for trusts needs to align with that of health authorities because of the inter-relationship between Trust finance and service strategies and those of purchasing authorities. Details of such plans are contained in Chapter 5, page 50: *Business Planning Process*.

The NHSE Outposts agree business plans and summaries for publication with Trusts. They collect annual, quarterly and monthly monitoring information from Trusts and agree corrective action as necessary.

The Outposts appraise business plans against a number of financial criteria before they are submitted to the NHSE.

Preparation of a business case

Since solutions that involve capital spending will introduce new capital charges with a long-term effect on NHS finances and prices, the first consideration of managers should be whether a capital solution is necessary. Where capital spending is the optimum solution, attention needs to be given to options that offset increased capital charges by releasing savings from land sales or reducing running costs. This presents opportunities to improve estate utilisation and also, through rationalisation, to reduce backlog maintenance.

Because the impact of capital investment is by nature long-term, it usually involves risk. Consequently, throughout the Business Case process, NHS managers will need to identify risks and consider strategies for managing them. These include not only risks that could arise to jeopardise the completion of the project according to plan, but also those that could result in the benefits of the investment not being obtained.

The preparation of a Business Case is the process that supports submissions for the funding of new capital projects. Underlying the presentation of a Business Case is the sound framework for option appraisal that has been required in the NHS for some time.

The Business Case process is divided into three phases, involving setting strategic direction and producing Outline and Full Business Cases. The three phases are depicted in the diagram below. The investment which the Business Case supports must meet a definable health need.

A Business Case must convincingly demonstrate that the project is economically sound, is financially viable and will be well managed. In addition a Business Case for any investment should show that the proposal has clearly identified benefits for patients and is supported by purchasers.

Preparing and presenting a robust business case can be costly: it may involve a great deal of management time to assess changing needs and conduct detailed analyses to identify a solution that considers costs, benefits and potential risks. It is therefore important to understand the process and plan for it carefully. It should clearly present value answers to the key questions:

- What services should be provided now and in the future?
- How will these service requirements be met in the most efficient and effective way?
- Why is capital spending proposed?
- Why does this proposal offer good value for money?
- How will the project be managed if the proposal is accepted?

Since April 1991, revenue accounts have been subject to capital charges for the use of assets and the question of capital charging is dealt with in Chapter 7.

6 ♦ *Financial and business planning*

Phase I

1. Set the strategic direction
   - Where are we now?
   - Where do we want to be?
   - Is the capital investment affordable?

Phase II

2. Define objectives and benefit criteria

3. Generate options

4. Measure the benefits

5. Identify and quantity the costs

6. Assess sensitivity to risk

● Review (Agree scope of work)

7. Identify the preferred option

8. Present the Outline Business Case

Review / recheck

Phase III

9. Produce the Full Business Case

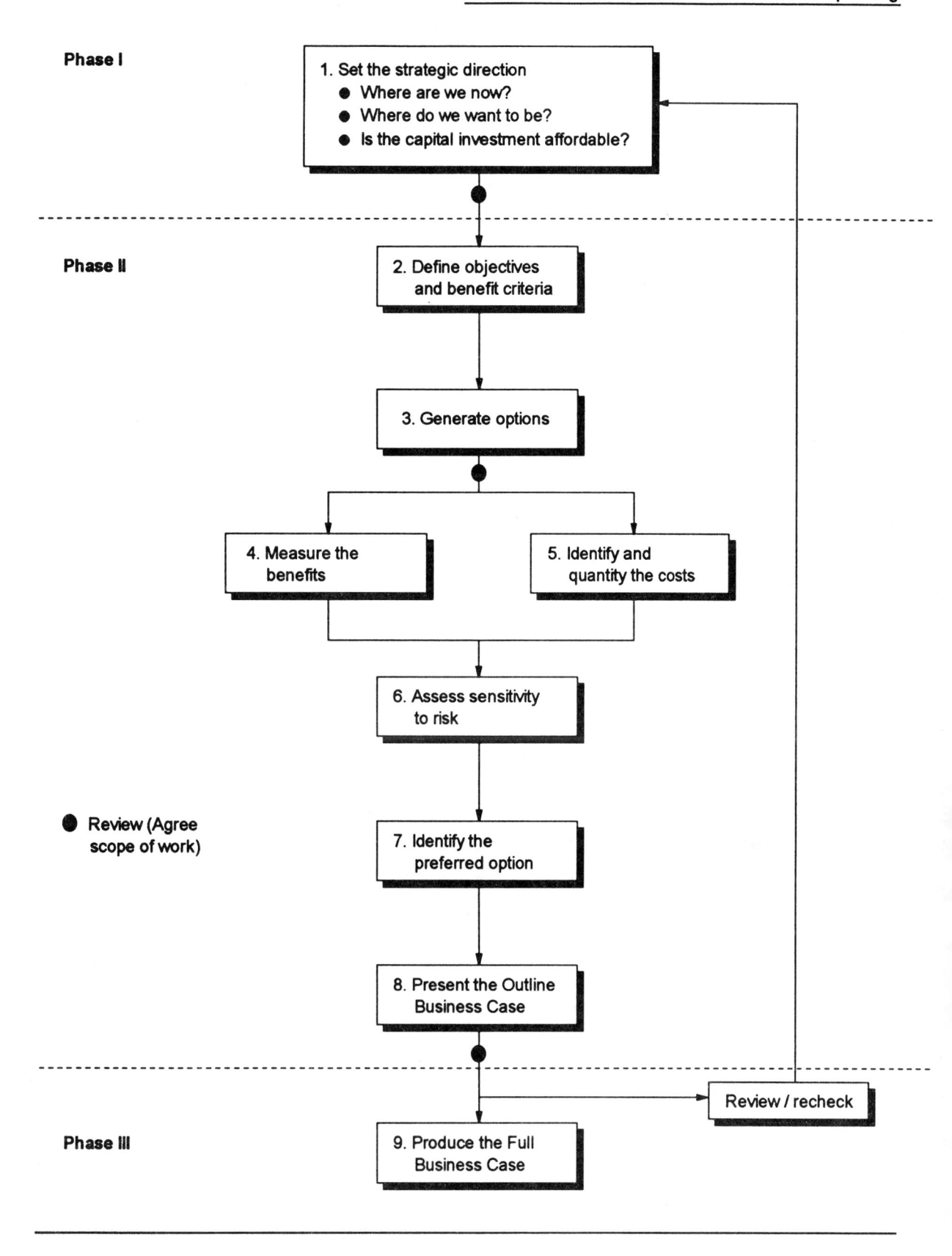

The Business Case Process

7

Capital expenditure and capital charges

Introduction and objectives

Since its inception in 1948 the NHS has received separate revenue and capital allocations. Once capital expenditure had been incurred no further revenue charges arose. On 1 April 1991, however the capital charges scheme came into operation, introducing charges for the use of capital assets. Local government is currently going through a similar process.

The objectives were:

- to increase the awareness of health service managers of the costs of capital;

- to provide incentives to use capital efficiently; and

- to ensure that capital charges are fully reflected in the pricing of hospital services, in order to promote fair competition within the NHS and also between the NHS and the private sector.

Capital charges enable contracts with NHS provider units to use prices which reflect the consumption of capital.

Scope and definition

Capital charges are payable on all assets which are owned by the NHS, except for assets acquired by gift (although not forming part of the capital charge, these are depreciated and charged as an expense).

The definition of a capital asset is 'tangible asset which is capable of being used in an authority's activities for a period which could exceed one year'.

In practice, capital expenditure comprises expenditure over £5,000 (increased from £1,000 on 1 April 1993) on:

- acquisition of land and premises;
- individual works schemes for the initial provision, extension, improvement, adaptation, upgrading, renewal, replacement or demolition of parts of the estate;
- items of equipment, including vehicles;
- costs of staff engaged on capital schemes.

Valuation of assets and asset lives

The operation of capital charging is dependent upon:

- an initial valuation of existing assets;
- an estimate of the length of life of assets.

Valuation of assets

- Land and buildings are valued by District Valuers every three years at their current value. Land and buildings held for operational use are valued at their open market value for existing use; those surplus to requirement are valued at open market value for alternative use. Values are indexed between the three year valuation.

- Other assets are valued at current cost, which is normally depreciated replacement cost.

Asset lives

Different types of assets have different life expectations, and are therefore depreciated over varying lengths of time. Authorities are required to work to nationally determined standard life expectancies eg:

Vehicles	7 years
Mainframe	8 years
Furniture	10 years
Engineering installations	5, 10 or 15 years
Main structures	up to 80 years maximum
Land	Permanent: not depreciated

At the inception of the system, assessment was made of the remaining life of all assets. Assessment of building structures was undertaken by the District Valuer who determined the remaining life based on the physical state of the buildings.

Assets are revalued on a current cost basis. The valuation of assets included on an authority's balance sheet will therefore show:

- value of assets at current cost replacement value, less
- depreciation to date,

and all assets are to be entered in a Fixed Asset Register which will record details of values and depreciation.

Capital charges calculations – depreciation and interest

Capital charges consist of two elements – depreciation and interest, and a distinction is made between DMUs and NHS Trusts.

Depreciation

The depreciation calculation for a financial year is based on the average value of assets during the year. This average is calculated by reference to the actual value of assets at the beginning of each quarter. This means that valuations need to be indexed each quarter and that depreciation is usually charged for complete quarters. There are two methods for calculating depreciation, one for assets subject to periodic revaluation and assessment of remaining life, ie. buildings and one for assets with a standard life, ie. equipment. Both methods are straight line.

Interest

Interest charges are based on the opening value of assets. In order to synchronise the calculation of depreciation and interest, the opening values used are the quarterly ones arrived at for the purposes of the depreciation calculation. The interest rate currently applicable to capital charges is 6% in real terms.

DMUs v NHS Trusts

Although the arrangements have been designed to ensure that there is common treatment of capital costs in the pricing of hospital services, there are important distinctions between DMUs and NHS Trusts in respect of capital charge payments.

These distinctions are as follows:

	DMU	NHS Trust
Depreciation	Payable to RHA and subsequently allocated to purchasers.	Depreciation is retained within the Trust. This together with accumulated surpluses will be one source of funding subject to its External Financing Limit for subsequent capital acquisitions.
Interest	Payable to RHA and subsequently allocated to purchasers.	Trusts do not make interest payments but are required to earn a target rate of return (6%) on the current value of their net assets.

Impact on resource allocation and pricing for contracts

Both elements of the capital charge are paid by DMUs to the RHA and form part of the allocation process. In the longer term it is intended that this will, as with revenue resources, be in accordance with a resident population based formula.

The funding flows for capital charges for DMUs are shown below. In respect of NHS Trusts, the arrangements for depreciation and interest outlined above ensure prices are calculated on a common basis. In order to provide additional finance to DHAs to purchase services from NHS Trusts (which is then partly financing Trust capital) the DoH transfers resources from capital to revenue which are added to the weighted capitation allocation.

The following diagram shows DMUs funding flows for capital charges. It illustrates how capital charges generated by DMUs, are 'recycled' to augment the annual revenue allocation from the Health Department to a RHA.

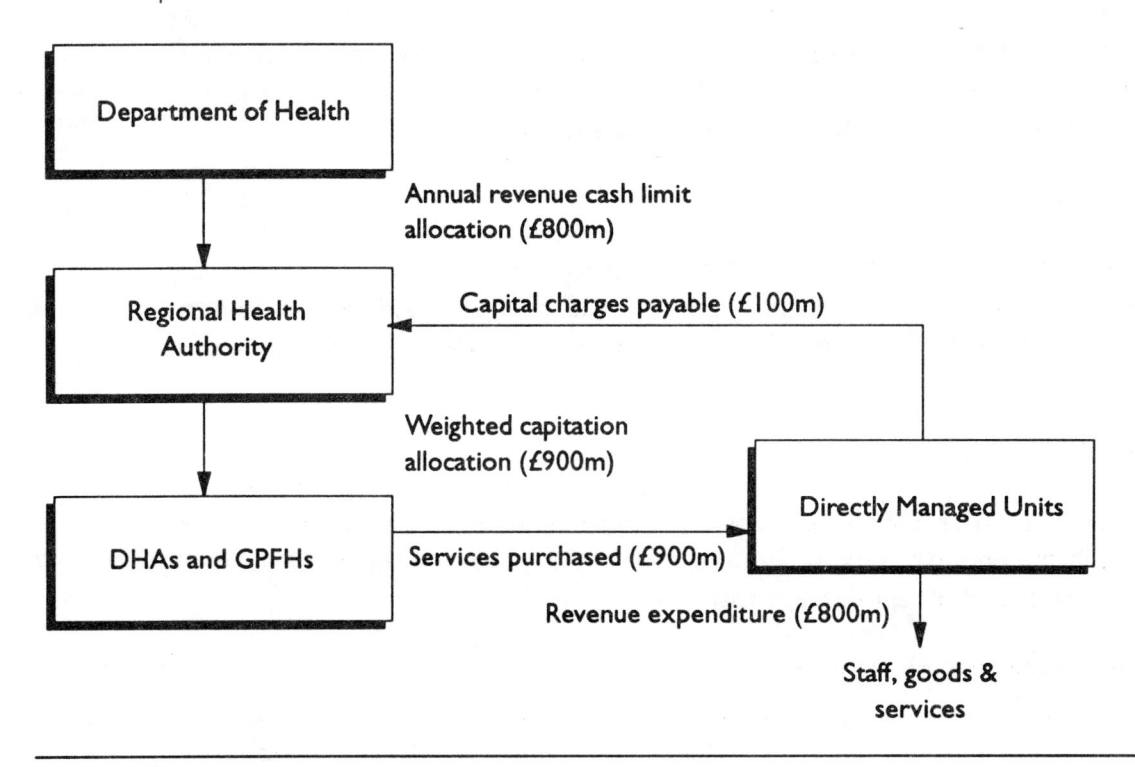

```
Department of Health
        |
        | Annual revenue cash limit
        | allocation (£800m)
        v
Regional Health  <----  Capital charges payable (£100m)  ----  
Authority                                                       |
        |                                                       |
        | Weighted capitation                                    |
        | allocation (£900m)                                     |
        v                                                   Directly Managed Units
DHAs and GPFHs  ----  Services purchased (£900m)  ---->
                      Revenue expenditure (£800m)  |
                                                   v
                                              Staff, goods &
                                                services
```

Accounting for capital charges

The main principles are as follows:

■ All assets (and groups of related assets) with a replacement value exceeding £5,000 and a useful life of more than one year are defined as capital items (this includes land and buildings, equipment, fixtures and fittings).

■ Who will pay capital charges? Directly managed hospitals will pay capital charges to RHAs for all their capital assets.

■ Exemption from capital charges – Gifts and certain Regional and District headquarters expenses (those which relate to the purchaser function) are to be exempt from capital charges.

■ Capital charges do not apply to NHS Trusts – Self-governing hospitals will not pay capital charges but will need to depreciate their assets and will have to achieve a specified revenue return on the value of their assets.

■ Land bears an interest charge but is not depreciated for.

- Maintaining a Fixed Assets Register – A register needs to be kept and updated for recording and valuing the authority's assets and calculating capital charges.

- Including of the cost of capital on budget statements – Charges for capital should be shown on revenue budget statements.

Why were capital charges introduced?

Under conventional bookkeeping principles, private sector companies depreciate their fixed assets. This is because although fixed assets are held for continued use, they will deteriorate with use and with time. Therefore, it would be wrong to continue reporting them in the accounts at their original cost.

It is, therefore, customary to provide for this loss in value by reducing the balance sheet value year by year over the life of the asset. These reductions are known as 'depreciation provisions'.

Historically, the NHS has not accounted for fixed assets (ie. not produced a balance sheet as part of its accounts which includes the value of its fixed assets). Therefore, authorities have had little idea of the extent and value of fixed assets held.

Moreover, until now there has been no incentive for health authorities to consider the financial consequences of their demand for more capital expenditure since there was no penalty for asking for more money for fixed assets.

The White Paper 'Working for Patient's' recognised this weakness in NHS accounting principles and from 1 April 1991 authorities have had to account for their assets.

DHA managed hospitals will therefore have to think carefully when they buy assets because the more assets they have, the higher capital charges they will have to pay.

The capital charge that DHA hospitals pay is a depreciation charge based on the current value of authorities' capital assets and an interest charge of a percentage of the current value of assets. The interest charge percentage is set by the Department of Health and is currently 6%.

DHA managed hospitals pay capital charges on capital assets such as:

- land and buildings;

- fixtures and fittings;

- equipment (eg. electro-medical, computing and catering).

Note that charges are not just paid on new assets; they are paid also on assets which hospitals owned before 1 April 1991.

Health authorities depreciate using 'replacement cost' rather than 'historic cost'. Replacement cost is known as 'current cost'. Set out below are examples of calculating depreciation on an historic cost basis and a replacement cost basis.

Depreciation based on historic cost

- Company X bought a van in 1988 for £7,000.
- In 1988, it is estimated that the van will last seven years.
- Company X estimates they will scrap the van for nothing in 1995.
- Therefore company X will lose £7,000 in seven years.
- It will cost Company X £1,000 (on average) each year because of depreciation.

This method of calculating depreciation is often called the 'straight line method'.

Depreciation (for 1991) based on replacement cost (current cost)

- Health Authority Y bought a van in 1988 for £7,000.
- It is estimated that the van will last for seven years and then be disposed of for nothing.
- In 1991, the price of vans has increased by 10% (ie. the replacement cost of the van is £7,000 + 10% = £7,700).
- Current cost depreciation for the year 1991/92 = £7,700 ÷ 7 = £1,100.
- Therefore, it will cost Health Authority Y £1,100 in real terms in 1991/92 because of depreciation.

From 1 April 1991 the NHS has used replacement costs to depreciate its assets. In order to calculate depreciation based on replacement cost, it is necessary to increase the replacement cost by an index relating to the price of that type of asset to arrive at the current replacement cost. This is then depreciated. The Department of Health (DoH) will provide hospitals with an index to take account of the increasing value of fixed assets over time. Finance Departments will need to use this index when calculating replacement cost depreciation charges. The assets' current replacement value and depreciation will be calculated quarterly.

NHS Trusts do not pay capital charges but they are subjected to similar controls because they will need to depreciate their assets. Their overall rate of return must take into account 'money lost' due to depreciation.

Any contract prices quoted by a self-governing hospital must take into account depreciation for the use that is made of capital assets. NHS Trusts do not pay their depreciation expense in cash. They have to pay an annual interest charge to the DoH and other lenders in respect of capital and repay interest on monies borrowed. When NHS Trusts were established, they paid an originating debt from the DoH to take account of the value of the NHS Trust's fixed assets.

A simple example to explain these principles would show:

> A NHS Trust hospital has bought a new operating microscope at a cost of £25,000. Its life time has been set at eight years.
>
> It is only used for cataract operations (200 per year). Staff, consumables and overheads for these operations in one year total £65,000.

A contract price for each cataract operation may be based on the following simple calculation:

		£
Staff and non pay expenditure	(£65,000 ÷ 200)	325.00
Cost of capital:		
(a) depreciation	(£25,000 ÷ 8 years) ÷ 200	15.63
(b) rate of return	(£25,000 × 6%) ÷ 200	7.50
Total costs		348.13

The principle is that each operation is not only charged for its share of the staff and consumables used but also for a share of the capital it uses. Note that the consultant should be charged on his budget not only staff and consumables but for also the cost of capital. In the above example the quarterly cost of capital is as follows:

	£
Depreciation (£25,000 ÷ 8 years) ÷ 4	781.25
Rate of return (£25,000 × 6%) ÷ 4	375.00
Cost of capital per quarter	1,156.25

DHA managed units will also incur an interest charge on the value of their assets. The interest rate is set by the Government, at 6%. The cost of capital represents the capital charge paid to the RHA (ie. £1,156.25 paid to the RHA per quarter). The capital charge of £23.13 (depreciation £15.63 + interest £7.50) will also be included in the contract price for each cataract operation.

Bookkeeping entries: general principles

There are a number of general principles governing the accounting entries necessary for capital charges. These are as follows:

- A prime objective of capital charges is to generate full costs of individual providers of health care. Separate accounts therefore need to be kept by directly managed units, district and special health authorities, family health services authorities and regional health authorities. These will include a balance sheet containing tangible assets.

- For health authorities only, the net assets in the balance sheet are represented by the following balances:

    - a capital account, identifying the modified historic cost of assets acquired and paid for by the authority;

    - a capital creditors account, identifying the net indebtedness of the authority in respect of capital expenditure;

    - a revaluation reserve, identifying movements in net assets valuations (eg. due to annual revaluations and indexation adjustments);

- a donation reserve, identifying the current net book value (including revaluation and indexation adjustments) of donated assets;

- a balance to/from Department, identifying net revenue working capital.

Capital charges accounting entries

The following accounts are required in general ledgers to accommodate the capital charge entries:

- In the books of Trusts, DMUs, district health authorities, family health services authorities and regional health authorities:

    tangible assets – land value
    tangible assets – building value
    tangible assets – equipment replacement cost
    tangible asset -equipment accumulated depreciation
    assets under construction
    capital account
    capital creditors account
    revaluation reserve
    donation reserve   ruction

- In addition to the above, the books of a DMU also require:

    non-cash settlement account to/from DHA
    inter-authority account to/from RHA
    capital acquisitions and disposals control account (note this is a suspense account)
    capital charges control account

The following accounting treatments should generally be used in the particular circumstances to which they relate:

1 Purchase of an asset

This is the basic entry in the accounts for the acquisition of assets. An asset may be acquired by a purchase or a transfer from another authority.

Dr	Tangible assets:		
	Either:	Equipment replacement cost	Value of
	Or:	Land or buildings valuation	the asset
Cr	Capital account		

Additions to assets under construction are accounted for in the same way.

2 Revaluation of assets

When assets are revalued the balances in the accounts have to be adjusted to the new value. The valuation adjustment equals the difference between the old depreciated value and the new valuation. The entries for the revaluation of property are shown below. There would be a similar adjustment to revalue the replacement cost and accumulated depreciation for other assets.

Dr	Tangible assets: Land and buildings valuation	Revaluation Adjustment
Cr	Revaluation reserve	

3 Indexation of assets

The following entry into the accounts gives the indexation applied to uplift the value of the asset:

Dr	Tangible assets: Either: Equipment replacement cost Or: Land and buildings valuation	Indexation
Cr	Revaluation reserve	

4 End of asset's depreciation life

When an equipment asset reaches the end of its standard depreciation life it is fully depreciated, giving a nil net book value. If it continues to be used no adjustment is made in the books and its costs and full depreciation continue to be carried (though the net of these two is nil), until it is no longer available for use.

Fully depreciated assets should continue to be recorded in the asset register.

No further capital charges arise.

Donated assets

Acquisition and depreciation

Assets acquired by way of donation after the establishment of the NHS on 5 July 1948 are not subject to capital charges. A donated asset is a capital asset, where the replacement value exceeds the capitalisation threshold, which has been acquired from non-exchequer sources. A donated asset may have been either received as a gift or purchased out of income received as a gift, where no consideration has been given in return. In cases where an asset has been partly funded as a donated asset, that proportion of the replacement cost of the asset which has been funded as a donation should be treated as a donated asset for accounting and capital charges purposes.

The recommended method for accounting for donated assets is outlined below. It is similar to one method approved for government grants in SSAP4. The principle is that the donation is treated as deferred income which is gradually released to meet the annual cost of depreciating the asset. This method is preferred because it records resources used at their full cost and matches income to expenditure.

- The donated asset is capitalised using the following entries:

Dr	Fixed asset replacement cost
Cr	Deferred donation

7 ♦ Capital expenditure and capital charges

- This is indexed annually. The following entries are used to post the indexation adjustment:

    Dr   Fixed asset replacement cost
    Cr   Deferred donation

- Similarly if an asset is revalued an adjustment is made to the deferred donation account. The revaluation reserve should not be used.

- When the asset is depreciated a charge is made to the revenue account:

    Dr   Depreciation revenue charge
    Cr   Fixed asset accumulated depreciation

- To pay for this income is released from the deferred donation account:

    Dr   Deferred donation
    Cr   Revenue income from donations

- As current cost accounting is being used backlog depreciation arises. This should not be charged to revenue. The following entries are made:

    Dr   Deferred donation
    Cr   Fixed asset accumulated depreciation

8

The contracting process

Introduction and types of contract

The separation of responsibility for purchasing and providing health care is an essential pre-requisite for the contracting process. The two roles may be summarised as follows:

- The Purchasing role – Districts have a primary responsibility to ensure that, within available resources, services are secured to meet the health needs of their resident populations. RHAs and GPFHs will also be purchasers of specific services. The Department of Health also acts as a purchaser in respect of overseas patients treated under reciprocal agreements and supra regional services, eg. heart and lung transplants.

- The Provider role – health care units deliver contracted services within quality and quantity specifications to one or a number of purchasers, in return for agreed charges. The provider units are, in the main, either Directly Managed Units or NHS Trusts.

Purchasers and providers thus enter into contracts, setting out the range and quality of services which a provider will deliver and the price which the purchaser will pay.

As a background to preparing contracts, the Purchaser will be concerned with an assessment of the Districts needs and the translation of those needs into service specifications and proposals. The Provider units will be primarily concerned with service provision proposals and how they fit into development plans. Discussion and negotiation between the two roles, before a patient care contract is prepared, will be mainly concerned with ensuring that income and expenditure commitments are acceptable within the financial and strategic plans of contracting bodies.

The particular elements relating to finance that are covered in this chapter are:

- types of contract;
- costing and pricing (covered in Chapter 9);
- invoicing, authorisation and settlement; and
- budgetary and financial control (including contract monitoring).

A separate section is devoted to regionally led contracting including education and training and the Service Increment for Teaching and Research (SIFTR). It should be noted that the remainder of this chapter is concerned with contracting for patient care services. There will be a wide range of contracts between health units for the provision of other services (for example laundry, financial services).

Types of patient care contract

There are three types of contract:

- BLOCK CONTRACTS, in which the provider is paid an annual sum in instalments, in return for access by the purchaser's residents to a defined range of services with limited volume specifications.

- COST AND VOLUME CONTRACTS, in which the provider receives a sum in return for treating a specified number of cases. There may also be a variable price per case component between a threshold and ceiling.

- COST PER CASE CONTRACTS, in which the purchaser agrees the price to be paid for the treatment of individual patients.

A proportion of patient referrals will not be predictable and hence not be covered by contracts. This proportion is normally small. These cases are known as extra contractual referrals (ECRs) and will be of two types: emergency and non-emergency (elective). Purchasers are obliged to pay for the emergency treatments but for the non-emergency cases the provider is required to obtain approval from the purchaser before treatment commences.

So far, the majority of contracts have been block, using indicative volumes for costing, pricing and monitoring purposes, but increasingly purchasers and providers are experimenting with more sophisticated cost and volume and cost per case contracts.

Payment arrangements

Invoicing

All services, whether under contract or extra contractual, have to be invoiced:

- Referrals under contract – in-patients

    - patient is admitted, and allocated to a contract. This is done by means of the postcode, which determines the district of residence, or in the case of GPFHs, the GPs list;

    - after discharge, patients notes have clinical codes attached to them to identify the type of treatment provided;

    - within one month of discharge an invoice must be sent to the purchaser for payment.

- Referrals under contract – all others

    Details as agreed within the contract must be fed into the finance department within a month of the event occurring, in order to prepare an invoice.

- Extra contractual referrals

    As above, except that for non-emergency (elective) ECR, the purchaser must provide an authorisation to pay.

Authorisation

It is the purchaser's responsibility to authorise requests for payment from providers. The exact nature of the authorisation will depend on the type of contract, although in all instances the principles of internal check and the separation of duties at key parts of the payments process should be applied.

Settlement

It is important that NHS purchasers settle payments to NHS providers promptly as failure to do so will present cash flow problems. A framework of rules has been developed, incorporating the following:

- monthly payments, payable in the second half of the month should be made for block contracts and for the fixed part of cost and volume contracts;

- for contracts where the total sum payable over a year varies with activity, parties should agree payment terms for the activity related element;

- for ECRs, payment should be made within one month of the date at which the invoice was sent (which itself should be within one month of the end of the month in which the episode of care ended). Where an episode of care is likely to extend over a long period, invoices may be submitted monthly;

- mechanisms for preventing delayed payment have been established eg. time limits specified for solving uncertainty about payments.

Financial control

This section is considered from the perspectives of the provider (whether DMU or NHS Trust) and District (as purchaser and manager of DMUs) respectively.

Provider unit control

- Budget setting

    Each provider will set budgets for income and expenditure.

    Income: the volume of work expected to be undertaken multiplied by the price for each item of service.

    Expenditure: A plan of what the hospital expects to spend in the following year in each functional or clinical area of the hospital.

    The volume of work should be that agreed within contracts plus the estimated number of extra contractual referrals. It is essential that the unit contains its expenditure within total anticipated income.

- Budgetary control

    Expenditure: actual expenditure incurred is compared and measured against the budget, both for the month concerned and cumulatively. Expenditure control and variance analysis is undertaken for each functional and/or clinical area. When variations are revealed, enquiries are made to ascertain the reasons for the variation and corrective measures determined.

    Income: actual income due is compared to the income budget and corrective action taken in respect of variations.

    Two types of variance may arise:

    - price variances: the volume of work anticipated is being achieved, but the prices have been set incorrectly: income is either higher or lower than budgeted;
    - volume variances: the volume of work anticipated is not being achieved or is being over-achieved.

    Contract monitoring will be undertaken by monthly contract reports which contain variance analysis.

District control

Health authorities have to manage at two levels:

- Cash: receipts and payments during the period 1 April to 31 March.
- Income and expenditure: expenditure incurred, and income received, relating to the financial year.

    The Department of Health requires Health Authorities not to exceed the cash limit. At a local level financial performance is reported on an income and expenditure basis as this reflects the actual level of resources consumed.

Regionally led contracting

In addition to receiving funds through payments by DHAs for services provided to their residents, provider units may also receive funds for specific purposes. These may include:

Service Increment for Teaching and Research (SIFTR)

A separate SIFTR contract will fund the costs of undergraduate medical and dental education and research in teaching hospitals. It is distributed to RHAs in proportion to undergraduate student numbers but paid directly to provider units to enable them to reduce their charges to DHAs and GPFHs, so that purchasers of services do not have to bear the cost of teaching and research in prices paid and hospitals which support teaching and research are not disadvantaged in pricing their services.

Education and training

The costs of training (mainly nursing and professions allied to medicine) are identified and removed from the prices charged by provider units to DHAs and GPFHs under contracts for services, as are 50% of the costs of junior doctors in training (from 1 April 1993). These training resources are then paid by the RHA to Colleges of Nursing and Midwifery and provider units.

9

Costing and pricing

Introduction and principles

In outlining the NHS Contracting Process, Chapter 8, page 73: '*Introduction and types of contract*', costing and pricing were identified as key financial elements of the internal market.

The process of costing is aimed at identifying and expressing the financial impact of a particular activity or the production of a particular unit of output. Within the NHS, costing has mainly been used for monitoring and comparison purposes, and has generally been based on historical information from prior year accounts. However, the new contractual arrangements between purchasers and providers of healthcare, and the importance of more clearly defining the NHS product, has increased the need for improved systems to establish prospective costs to enable prices to be set.

The link between prices, essential in any contractual arrangement, and cost is fundamental, especially as the basic approach to pricing set out in DoH guidance is that:

- prices should be based on costs;

- prices should generally be arrived at on a full cost basis (marginal costing is only allowed where there is spare capacity for a short-term period); and

- there should be no planned cross subsidisation.

In order for the internal market to operate it is essential that prices reflect cost differences between providers ie. prices should be based on the costs of the provider concerned rather than, for example, regional or national average costs for specific services.

Each provider needs to match income to expected expenditure (and the financial target for NHS Trusts) through the contracting process. It will therefore be necessary to make assumptions about the service levels the hospital will be providing (which, in turn, will be based on assumptions about the volume of work which will be won through contracts) and to plan to ensure that all costs are recovered through the prices set for those contracts and any extra contractual work which is expected to be carried out.

In order to be effective in supporting the internal market, it is essential that any costing approach adopted should operate consistently, in terms of the overall principles on which it is based, within and between individual units. If this is not the case management decisions within both purchaser and provider organisations may be based on incorrect information.

It is desirable that the costing approach takes account of other uses of costing information (besides contract pricing) so that managers are not faced with the task of running different management information systems for different people.

Reconciliation of costing information with the devolved management budget or control total of planned income and expenditure is essential in order to validate the costing information in total, to ensure that overall financial control is maintained and to plan to ensure that all costs are recovered.

As the contracting system develops and matures requirements will change. Budget holders will become more informed about individual contractors' use of resources, service providers will become more sophisticated in pricing contracts and purchasers will become more demanding in specifying and monitoring contracts. The costing and pricing arrangements must be capable of changing and developing to meet these requirements and to move, over time, from what may initially be limited and relatively simple approaches, to a position where high quality information systems are available to facilitate the pricing of contracts.

Costing techniques

A number of different approaches to 'product' costing are currently in use in commercial organisations. All of them could have applications in costing hospital services, although only some of them are appropriate to support contract pricing.

Direct costing is not a full cost approach and is therefore inappropriate for setting contract prices.

Total absorption costing overcomes this weakness because indirect and overhead costs are 'absorbed' into product costs using allocation or apportionment techniques. Prices can then be set on the basis of full costs. However there are two factors in this approach which need to be recognised when setting prices; the procedures for overhead absorption into 'product' costs may be arbitrary and total cost per unit will only be correct at the 'sales' volume assumed at the time of calculating overhead absorption rates, ie. if actual volumes are greater or less than the assumed volume, fixed costs will be over or under recovered respectively.

The marginal cost approach focuses on those costs which are variable with the volume of output produced. Other costs are treated as fixed or 'period' costs. Marginal costing is appropriate for setting prices for the sale of spare capacity where the costs of increasing output may be limited to the cost of additional materials used because labour costs are already paid or committed for the period in question.

Standard costing can be integrated with either a total absorption or a marginal costing approach. Essentially it is a control mechanism. As its name implies, the approach establishes technical and costs standards for each process in order to establish not only what a product will cost, but also what it ought to cost. Comprehensive standard costing systems are not appropriate for the NHS contracting environment. However, establishing some simple standard costs in certain areas may be helpful in building up a procedure cost, for example. This type of standard costs are already being used by resource management sites.

Activity based costing is not so much a new approach to costing as a means of refining the procedures for overhead cost absorption. The approach taken is to examine the activities undertaken in each department in order to identify the true 'cost drivers' and then use these as the means of absorbing indirect costs into product costs. In the commercial and manufacturing sectors, for example, overhead costs have traditionally been attributed to 'products' on the basis of the direct labour hours or direct materials cost for the product concerned. The activity based costing approach identified suitable activity measures for each overhead department and then uses these to attribute the costs for that department to products.

In summary the techniques appropriate for costing most contracts in the NHS are total absorption costing using activity based costing for absorption of overheads. Marginal costing will be important to support decisions about the sale of spare capacity and simple standard costs may be helpful in building up individual procedure costs.

Cost allocation framework

The framework has a number of elements, including the identification of costs and income, making assumptions about the level of service to be provided and the number and type of contracts expected and finally attributing costs and income to contracts. This approach is not intended to be prescriptive. Each provider unit will need to develop its own framework.

In order to attribute costs to individual contracts assumptions about service levels are required. A planned level of capacity and volume of service for individual sites of departments needs to be established, in order that, at the price set, the budgeted level of service will recover all costs.

Attributing costs to services and contracts requires that costs are classified and analysed in order to identify the direct, indirect, overhead and capital charge elements and the fixed, semi-variable and variable components. This is a complicated task. Classification and analysis will need to vary from one unit to another in order to reflect local circumstances, and the sophistication of existing information systems. The analysis of costs into their fixed, semi-fixed and variable components will depend on the individual circumstances in which the information is being used.

Establishing total costs

Total costs will be the sum of the following elements:

- direct patient treatment costs;

- indirect and overhead costs;

- costs of services received from the DHA or RHA;

- capital costs – depreciation and interest for directly managed units and depreciation plus the financial rate of return for a NHS trust;

- other costs, eg. teaching or research costs which relate to the delivery of clinical services;

- offsetting SIFT revenue, donations, revenue from income generation schemes, use of trust funds to meet revenue service costs, income earned from other units, eg. for pathology services and miscellaneous income, eg. shops.

This gives a total of net costs which must be recovered through income from contracts and extra contractual referrals.

In establishing total costs, individual providers will need to satisfy themselves that they can produce a reasonable estimate of all these costs and revenues. Although historic information may provide a starting point, this will need to be rolled forward, taking account of planned workload changes and likely pay and price increases, in order to provide prospective costs as the basis for contract prices.

Levels of service

The assumed level of service is the total level of service expected to be provided in the forthcoming year on which total costs are to be recovered at the prices set.

It is a key element in estimating prospective costs and attributing these to contracts. If the level is set too low, prices will be unnecessarily high; if too high, costs may not be fully recovered. It will therefore be necessary to make assumptions about patient activity levels at specialty level and probably procedure level in certain areas. It will also be necessary to make assumptions about activity levels in all hospital departments, eg. pathology and radiology requests, as a basis for allocating these costs to specialties.

If the costing and pricing process is starting from historic specialty cost information, it will be important to understand how these costs behave if the assumed level of service in any particular area is significantly different from historic levels. This requires an analysis of costs into their fixed, semi-fixed and variable components.

The assumed level of service will be greater than the volume of service covered by contracts in place at the start of the year, whether these be with DHAs or GP practice fundholders. The difference will be accounted for by contracts entered into during the course of the year and by extra contractual referrals in year.

Quality assumptions should also be reflected in the assumed level of service, eg. length of stay.

Cost attribution

Costs may be attributed to activity at a number of different levels, eg. patient, procedure, diagnostic related groups (DRG) or Specialty. Requirements will be determined by detailed contract specifications.

In most cases, specialty based contracts will be the norm, though procedure based contracts may be appropriate in certain areas.

Specifying contracts at DRG level would present costing difficulties that would need to be handled sensitively. For example:

- although the provider may be able to classify its output in this way, particularly when resource management systems become more developed, it may not be an appropriate way for all purchasers to specify needs – GP fundholders, for example, may be unfamiliar with these categories;

- given the large number of DRGs, individual providers may have only a small number of patients in many groups, this may produce unreliable average costs which differ significantly from year to year and from those of other providers;

- DRGs do not cover outpatients or long-stay patients.

Cost classification and analysis

Having established the total cost and the assumed level of service the next step is to classify and analyse costs in order to facilitate the attribution of costs to contracts. Cost may be classified or analysed as illustrated above. Items of income, eg. SIFT could be classified or analysed in a similar way. These two approaches may be used separately, but a more flexible approach would be to integrate them, so that for example, direct costs could be analysed into their fixed, semi-fixed and variable components.

The first task is to classify costs as to whether they are 'direct' treatment costs, eg. medical and nursing staff costs or drugs; 'indirect' treatment costs, eg. catering, laundry and linen; overhead costs, eg. management and administration and estate management costs or capital charges.

The sophistication of available information systems will determine the level or costing detail that can be achieved, eg. specialty or patient. Having made that decision direct costs will be attributed directly, indirect cost can be allocated using units of activity appropriate to the department concerned and overhead costs can be apportioned on some relatively simple basis, eg. patient days. Capital costs should where possible be identified to the relevant 'facility' (eg. ward or theatre) or department using the assets. In this way they can be either attributed directly to the specialty concerned (if for example, a ward is used exclusively by one specialty) or allocated to specialties along with the other costs of the department concerned, eg. laundry.

If unplanned spare capacity arises within a particular year, it may be 'sold' at a price which represents marginal or variable cost. In this situation it is therefore necessary to understand the fixed, semi-fixed and variable components of costs. Fixed costs would be excluded when setting prices, while all variable costs would be included. Each item of semi-fixed cost would need to be considered separately as to how it would be affected by the proposed contract. Each time the opportunity to sell spare capacity arises the analysis of costs into their fixed, semi-fixed and variable components will be influenced by the size and duration of the proposed contract.

Following the allocation or apportionment of all costs and relevant income to specialities, costs will need to be attributed to individual contracts on the basis of assumed levels of service so that the budgeted level of service will recover all costs at the prices set.

It is therefore necessary, to divide the total assumed level of service between the individual contracts (with either DHAs or GPs) which the provider expects to enter into, and the extra contractual work which it expects to do in year. This will provide a framework for attributing costs and income to individual contracts (see Chapter 7, page 66: 'Accounting for Capital Charges').

National Steering Group on Costing (NSGC)

The NHSE had some concern during 1991/92 and 1992/93 about the wide variations in prices charged for seemingly like services across the country. A National Steering Group on Costing (NSGC) was therefore established to examine costing for contracting.

The NSGC has endorsed the Cost Allocation Principles first explained in EL(90)173, 'Cost Allocation Principles'. The guidelines allowed a large degree of discretion in the detailed methods that a provider can adopt in their cost allocation and apportionment methods, provided that the methods conform to the basic pricing policy which can be stated as:

> 'Price must be based on full (net) costs so that, for a provider's annual assumed volume of service, income from contracts (and ECRs) will recover the quantum of cost with no planned cross subsidisation between contracts'.

The NSGC has now recommended a minimum standard that all providers should reach in analysing costs in their fixed, semi-fixed and variable elements and classifying them into direct, indirect and overhead. Providers are strongly encouraged to develop methods of attributing cost directly to specialty where possible and to use the minimum standard method of apportionment between specialties when required.

The NSGC has re-stated the need for the sharing of information between provider and purchaser, thereby better informing the contracting process.

'Cost allocation: General Principles and Approach for 1993/94' published by the NHSE in April 1993 contained full details of this approach and during the financial year 1993/94 use of sub-specialty costs bands was tested at several pilot sites around the country.

Revised arrangements for the 1994/95 contracting round were published by the NHSE in August 1993 (FDL(93)59).

Unit costing

Health authorities produce a wide range of patient and workload statistics and unit costs are developed from these.

Financial Return HFR21 (see Chapter 10, page 87: *Annual accounts and financial returns*') lists the following services and units of work measurement.

9 ♦ Costing and pricing

A	Patient treatment services	Unit of work measurement (see below)
A1		
(a)	Wards	a
(b)	Out-patient clinics	b
(c)	Day care facilities	b
(d)	A and E departments	b
(e)	Community Medical Services	c
(f)	Community Nursing & Midwifery Services	c
(g)	Community Dental Services	s
A2		
(a)	Artificial Limb & Wheelchair Services	d
(b)	Audiology	b
(c)	Chiropody	e
(d)	Dietetics	e
(e)	Electrocardiography	f
(f)	Electroencephalography	g
(g)	Health education/promotion	s
(h)	Industrial therapy	b
(i)	Lithotripsy	b
(j)	Medical illustration and photography	*
(k)	Medical physics	*
(l)	Misc patient treatment services	*
(m)	Nuclear medicine	f
(n)	Occupational therapy	e
(o)	Operating theatres	h
(p)	Optical services	e
(q)	Pathology:	
	(i) Chemical pathology	g
	(ii) Cytogentics	g
	(iii) Haematology	g
	(iv) Histopathology	g
	(v) Immunology	g
	(vi) Microbiology	g
	(vii) Spare	–
	(viii) Spare	–
(r)	Patient transport service (non emerg)	i
(s)	Pharmacy	j
(t)	Physiotherapy	k
(u)	Psychology	k
(v)	Radiology	f – 100
(w)	Radiotherapy departments	l
(x)	Speech therapy	e
	TOTAL A	

9 ♦ Costing and pricing

B	Unit/Estate support services	Unit of work measurement (see below)
B1		
(a)	Domestic	m
(b)	Catering	n
(c)	Laundry/Linen	o
(d)	Portering/Transport	o
(e)	Engineering maintenance	p
(f)	Building maintenance	p
(g)	Energy/Water and Sewerage	*
(h)	Community Dental Services	*
	TOTAL B1	-
B2		
(a)	General manager	q
(b)	Unit Office Support	q
(c)	Employee services	r
(d)	Procurement of goods and services	q
(e)	Medical records	o
	TOTAL B2	
B3	Training education	*
B4	Miscellaneous	*
	TOTAL A + B	-
	Add: Purchase of tertiary referrals	-
	GRAND TOTAL (S/C 200 + S/C 210)	

Units of work measurement:

(a) patient day
(b) attendance
(c) 1,000 resident population served by this community service
(d) item issued
(e) face to face contact
(f) weighted request
(g) request
(h) operating tour
(i) patient journey
(j) £1,000 expenditure on drugs
(k) first contact
(l) exposure
(m) 100 sq metres cleaned

(n)   1,000 occupied bed days plus 40% of day care attendances
(o)   1,000 weighted occupied bed days
(p)   building volume (100 cubic metres)
(r)   1 person employed (WTE)
(s)   1,000 resident population served.
*   There is no unit of work measurement

Performance indicators

Performance indicators have been collected on a national basis since the early 1980s. Health authorities are required to submit statistical returns to the Department of Health and also to publish performance indicators as part of their annual report.

The Department of Health uses the statistics to manage, plan and review the activities and performance of health authorities.

Performance indicators are essentially of two types: cost and intermediate.

The use of unit costs as a performance indicator is widespread in all public sector organisations. It is the basic indicator and health authorities calculate unit costs for nearly all their activities. Some examples are:

- cost per in-patient day;
- cost per out-patient attendance;
- cleaning costs per square metre;
- nursing costs per in-patient day;
- pharmacy costs per in-patient.

Health authority managers use unit costs as a basis for planning, controlling and reviewing the various activities and services they manage. Within health authorities unit costs are produced for individual wards, operating theatres and specialisms such as occupational theory – managers are therefore able to monitor and compare the performance of wards and specialisms.

Intermediate performance indicators are also used as a basis for planning, controlling and reviewing activities. They support the unit cost indicators. Some examples are as follows:

- bed occupancy rates;
- average waiting times for hospital treatment (split between specialisms or illness);
- operating theatre usage rate;
- percentage of day cases;
- average length of stay.

10

Final accounts and returns

Introduction

This chapter sets out the principal requirements for final accounts, supporting statements and financial returns, which are then considered in practice on page 100: *'Statements of Standard Accounting Practice'*.

Annual accounts and financial returns

The purpose of the accounts is to satisfy the 'primary requirements of public accountability for the use of NHS financial resources', including performance against the parliamentary vote. The annual accounts are used as the basis for the summarised accounts which the NHSE is required to prepare and submit to the Comptroller and Auditor General who examines these accounts, certifies them and lays copies of them, together with his report, before Parliament.

The accounts must be accompanied by a statement of accounting practice and must be certified by the Director of Finance and acknowledged by the Chairman prior to audit. The required date for completion of the annual accounts is the 30 June after the financial year to which they relate.

As a general rule DHAs and NHS Trusts are expected to prepare annual accounts in accordance with accounting standards issued or adopted by the Accounting Standards Board (ASB). The annual accounts of both DHAs and NHS Trusts are integrated documents comprising three main statements supported by a series of notes to the accounts.

The three main statements are:

- Income and Expenditure Account;
- Balance sheet;
- Cash flow statement.

A series of supporting notes augment these summary statements. In addition to the annual accounts, DHAs and NHS Trusts are required to complete a set of financial returns to provide various analyses of expenditure which are not obtainable from the annual accounts. Details are given on pages 91 *Supporting notes* and 93 *Financial returns*.

Income and expenditure accounts

District Health Authority

This reports separately on the purchasing and managing roles of the District Health Authority, as follows:

INCOME		
Allocations		Cash drawn from revenue cash limit allocation
Miscellaneous income		Income generation etc
TOTAL INCOME	X	
EXPENDITURE		
Health care and related services purchased		Services purchased for resident population
Authority administration and purchasing expenses		Costs of the purchasing function
Other services expenditure		Eg. Joint Finance, Care in the Community
Community Health Councils		
TOTAL EXPENDITURE	X	
Net revenue operating surplus /deficit of DMUs	X	Net income/expenditure of all DMUs
Net revenue operating surplus /deficit of common services	(X)	Net income/expenditure of all common services
Surplus/deficit for the financial year	X	

NHS Trusts

The NHS Trust Income and Expenditure account is more akin to a standard commercial profit and loss account, as follows:

Income from activities	X	Income from HAs, GPFHs, NHS Trusts, DoH and Non NHS bodies for patient care.
Other operating income	X	Patient transport service, income generation, Charitable contributions, etc
	X	
Operating expenses	X	
OPERATING SURPLUS	X	
Interest receivable	X	Interest received on cash investments.
Interest payable	X	Interest payable on: Originating interest Bearing debt and further borrowing.
SURPLUS ON ORDINARY ACTIVITIES	X	
Extraordinary items	X	Defined as in SSAP6
SURPLUS FOR FINANCIAL YEAR	X	
PDC dividends payable	X	
RETAINED SURPLUS FOR YEAR	X	
Prior year adjustment	X	
Surplus carried forward	X	

Balance sheets

This is a statement of the assets and liabilities at the beginning and end of the financial year.

District health authority

Fixed assets
    Land
    Buildings   } Net book value, ie. after indexation,
    Equipment   }   revaluation, depreciation
    Assets under construction

Total

Current assets
    Stocks and work in progress   Not patient services
    Debtors
    Cash at bank and in hand
    Sub-total
    Creditors – amounts falling due   ie. to other NHS bodies, income tax
        within one year   and social securities, other creditors
    Net current assets/liabilities
    Creditors – amounts falling due   Any liabilities not payable until more
        after more than one year   than 12 months after the Balance sheet date

    Total net assets   X

Financed by:
    Capital account   Represents assets purchased using NHS funds
    Donation reserve   Represents the value of assets acquired
                                                  by donation post-1948
    Balance due to/from Department of   Difference between total assets and
        Health   total liabilities and the balance on the
                                                  capital account

Total   X

NHS Trust

Fixed assets   As DHA

Current assets
Stocks & work in progress
Debtors
Short term investments
Cash at bank and in hand
Creditors (due within one year)   As DHA
Net current liabilities
Total assets less current liabilities
Creditors (due after one year)   As DHA

Total assets employed   X

Financed by:
Public dividend capital
Long-term loans
Revaluation reserve   Represents change in valuation of fixed assets.
Donation reserve   As DHA
Other reserves
Income and expenditure account   Surplus carried forward

Total   X   = Total assets employed

A more detailed example is given in Chapter 9.

Cash flow statement

The cash flow statement restates the information that is given in the balance sheet and income and expenditure account, to give particular emphasis to the source and application of funds.

Supporting notes

DHAs

A series of supporting notes give more detail on a number of aspects of Authorities' financial performance:

Notes to the Income and Expenditure Account

Note 2.1	—	Source of Health care purchased	—	Own DMUs
			—	Other DMUs
			—	NHS Trusts
			—	Other providers
Note 2.2	—	Authority administration, purchasing, other services, CHCs
Note 2.3	—	Authority members' remuneration
Note 2.4	—	Staff costs

Accounts of DMUs and Common Services
- Note 3.1 — Net revenue operating surplus or deficit of DMUs
- Note 3.2 — Income from patient services (analysed by source)
- Note 3.3 — Other operating income
- Note 3.4 — Operating expenses (analysed subjectively ie. by type of expense)
- Note 4   — Net revenue operating surplus or deficit of common services
  - The principle of maximum devolution of services to operational level has resulted in the emergence of a range of activities that are managed centrally to provide support services to units. These include ambulance and patient transport services managed at Regional or District level

10 ♦ Final accounts and returns

Notes to the Balance Sheet
Note 5.1 – Fixed assets – analysis showing additions, disposals and revaluations
Note 5.2 – Stocks and work in progress
Note 5.3 – Debtors
Note 5.4 – Creditors – amounts falling within one year
Note 5.5 – Creditors – amounts falling due after more than one year
Note 5.6 – Patients money – Statement of custodianship of funds held on behalf of patients in care of the Authority
Note 5.8 – Contingent liabilities
Items not included in the accounts but for which uncertainty exists (eg. claims for medical negligence, third party claims and bad debts)
Note 5.9 – Post balance sheet events
– A narrative giving details of the event with an estimate of the financial effect
Note 5.10 – Capital commitments
– Contract commitments or recorded decisions which will lead to capital spending in future years
Note 5.11 – Balances with the Department of Health, Health Authorities, Family Health Services Authorities and NHS Trusts
Note 5.12 – Balance sheet analysis by Headquarters, Directly Managed Unit and Common Services

NHS Trusts

A series of supporting notes give more detail on a number of aspects of NHS Trusts' financial performance:

Note 1 – Accounting policies

Notes to the Income and Expenditure Account
Note 2 – Income from activities
Note 3 – Other operating income
Note 4 – Operating expenses
Note 5 – Staff details
Note 6 – Interest receivable
Note 7 – Interest payable
Note 8 – Extraordinary items
Note 9 – Financial target performance

Notes to the Balance Sheet
Note 10 – Intangible fixed assets
Note 11 – Tangible fixed assets
Note 12 – Stocks and work in progress
Note 13 – Debtors
Note 14 – Short term investments
Note 15 – Creditors
Note 16 – Short term loans
Note 17 – Public dividend capital
Note 18 – Long-term loans
Note 19 – Movements on reserves

Other notes to the Financial Statements
Note 20 – External financial limit
Note 21 – Capital commitments
Note 22 – Post balance sheet events
Note 23 – Contingent liabilities
Note 24 – Pensions
Note 25 – Clinical negligence

Financial returns

The financial returns, as required for the financial year 1992/93, are as follows:

DHA ref	Title
FR4 –	Catering
FR5 –	Laundry
FR6 –	Laundry and linen services
FR16 –	Patient transport services
FR19 –	Purchase of Health Care from non-NHS bodies and grants to voluntary bodies
FR20 –	Joint Finance and Care in the Community
FR21 –	Hospital and Community Health Services Dept. Analysis
FR22 –	Specialty and programme costs
FR23 –	Administration and purchasing expenses
FR24 –	Care Group Analysis of Health Services purchased
FR25 –	Analysis of expenditure by type (subjective analysis)
FR26 –	Analysis of stocks
FR27 –	Fixed assets
FR28 –	Artificial limb and wheelchair services
RP5 –	Losses and special payments

Annual accounts in practice

NHS Manual of Accounts

The NHS Executive's *'NHS Manual for Accounts'* lays down the format of the accounting statements produced by the various tiers of the Health Service.

The Accounting Statements

Each RHA and DHA is required to produce an **income and expenditure account**, a **balance sheet** and a **cash flow statement**. These annual financial statements are supplemented by very detailed notes and financial returns as indicated on pages 91 *'Supporting notes'* and 93 *'Financial returns'* of this Chapter.

The latest edition of the *'NHS Manual for Accounts'* sets out the requirements for final accounts in great detail and to reproduce those requirements in this Book would result in several additional volumes. What this section therefore does, is to summarise the contents of the *NHS Manual for Accounts* and then give examples of the three main accounting statements.

In local government parlance, the Manual is equivalent to a combination of CIPFAs 1993 Accounting Code of Practice, (which sets out the format of annual accounts to be published) and CIPFAs separate publications, 'The Standard Form of Published Accounts' and the 'Standard Classification of Income and Expenditure', which provide the detail behind the Code of Practice. The NHS requirements are, however, far more prescriptive, although CIPFAs Code of Practice requirements are intended to be a minimum. Thus, there is absolute standardisation of the format of the accounts of each health authority – an important ingredient to ensure central consistency and uniformity; when the NHS Executive summarises all the return for audit and subsequent report to Parliament.

Summary of the NHS Manual for Accounts

Chapter	Contents
2	Submission of annual accounts and financial returns
3	NHS Accounting Standards
4	General principles for assigning income and expenditure
5	Prompt closure of accounts
6	The receipts and payments returns
7	The Health Authority Annual Accounts
8	Annual Accounts of Charitable (Trust) Funds and Special Trustees
9	The Financial Returns (FR forms)

Format of the Main Statements

These now follow:

ACCOUNTS 19. . . . .

. . . . HEALTH AUTHORITY	AUTHORITY CODE		

Revenue income and expenditure

for the year ended 31 March 19. . . .

19. . . .		SUB CODE	MAINCODE 06
£	**INCOME** Allocations	100	£
	Miscellaneous income	100	
	TOTAL	140	
	EXPENDITURE Health care and related services purchased (see note 2.1)	150	
	Authority administration and purchasing expenses	160	
	Other services expenditure	170	
	Community Health Councils	180	
	Subtotal (see note 2.2)	190	
	TOTAL REVENUE EXPENDITURE	200	
	Net revenue operating surplus or deficit of Common Services (see note 3.1)	210	
	Net revenue operating surplus or deficit of Common Services (see note 4)		
	Surplus (deficit) for the financial year	250	

10 ♦ Final accounts and returns

ACCOUNTS 19. . . . .

.... HEALTH AUTHORITY   AUTHORITY CODE ☐☐☐

Balance Sheet as at 31 March 19. . . .

19. . . .		SUB CODE	MAINCODE 07
£	**FIXED ASSETS** Net book value: Land	100	£
	Buildings	110	
	Equipment	120	
	Assets under construction	130	
	TOTAL (see note 5.1)	140	
	CURRENT ASSETS Stocks and work in progress (see note 5.2)	150	
	Debtors (see note 5.3)	160	
	Cash at bank and in hand	170	
	Subtotal	180	
	Creditors: amounts falling due within one year (see note 5.4)	190	
	Net current assets/liabilities	200	
	Creditors: amounts falling due after more than one year (see note 5.5)	210	
	Total net assets	220	
	FINANCED BY: Capital account (see note 5.7)	230	
	Donation reserve (see note 5.7)	240	
	Balance due to/(from) Department	250	
	TOTAL	260	

The net book value of land and buildings at 31 March 19... comprises:

  Freehold
  Long leasehold
  Short leasehold

  Total

10 ♦ Final accounts and returns

ACCOUNTS 19. . . . .

.... HEALTH AUTHORITY   AUTHORITY CODE

Source and Application of Funds Statement for the year ended 31 March 19. . . .

19. . . .		SUB CODE	MAINCODE 08
£	**SOURCE OF FUNDS** Cash limit: Revenue	100	£
	Capital	110	
	TOTAL CASH LIMIT	120	
	Other sources of funds: Miscellaneous income	130	
	Proceeds from the sale of fixed assets	140	
	Charitable and other contributions to capital expenditure	150	
	Total sources of funds	160	
	APPLICATIONS OF FUNDS Revenue expenditure	200	
	Net revenue operating (surplus) or deficit of directly managed units	210	
	Net revenue operating (surplus) or deficit of common services	220	
	Additions to fixed assets	230	
	Total application of funds	240	
	CHANGE IN WORKING CAPITAL Stocks and work in progress	300	
	Net balances with Department of Health, Health Authorities, Family Health Services Authorities and NHS Trusts	310	
	Other debtors	320	
	Other creditors	330	
	Cash at bank and in hand	340	
	Total change in working capital	350	
	Under/(over) spending against cash limit	360	
	Analysed as: Revenue	370	
	Capital	380	
	TOTAL	390	

10 ♦ Final accounts and returns

This degree of detail would not be required in an examination question, so an 'abridged' form is shown in the following example in which capital charges are included:

DHA Balances at 31 March 19...

	£'000
Land (book value)	8,000
Buildings (less depreciation £2,000,000)	58,000
Equipment (less depreciation £150,000)	2,348
Stocks	358
Debtors	54
Creditors	170
Cash overdrawn	390
Capital account	60,000
Donation reserve	6,000
Cash-limited allocation	78,000
Miscellaneous income	12,200
Community Health Council	1,000
Purchase of health care and other related services	60,000
Other services expenditure	17,400
Administration	10,400
DMUs operating deficit	2,600
Common services operating deficit	1,000

Income and expenditure account for the year ended 31 March 19...

	£'000	£'000
Income		
Allocation	78,000	
Miscellaneous income	12,200	
Total income		90,200
Expenditure		
Health care and other related services purchased	60,000	
Administration	10,400	
Other services expenditure	17,400	
Community Health Council	1,000	
Total expenditure		88,800
Net income		1,400
DMUs – net operating deficit		(2,600)
Common services – net operating deficit		(1,000)
Deficit for the financial year		2,200

Balance sheet as at 31 March 19...

	£'000	£'000	£'000
Fixed assets (see note below)			
Land		8,000	
Buildings		58,000	
Equipment		2,348	
			68,348
Current assets			
Stocks	358		
Debtors	54		
		412	
Less: Current liabilities			
Creditors	170		
Cash overdrawn	390		
		560	
			(148)
			68,200
Financed by:			
			£'000
Capital account			60,000
Donation reserve			6,000
Accumulated deficit			2,200
			68,200

Note.

Fixed assets

	Land £'000	Buildings £'000	Equipment £'000
At valuation	8,000	60,000	2,498
Less: Depreciation	-	2,000	150
Book value	8,000	58,000	2,348

Statements of Standard Accounting Practice

The Secretary of State for Health expects that health authorities will follow SSAPs and Financial Reporting Statements where relevant, in the compilation of their annual accounts. There is a similar general requirement for NHS Trusts.

Present NHS accounting standards update and replace the previous standards which were implemented from financial year 1983/84. Draft revisions to those standards were proposed following a Departmental internal review in 1990 and agreed following wide consultation. During the process of revision, account was taken of comments from the then Consultative Committee of the Accounting Bodies on the original NHS standards, new and amended commercial standards and specific relevant developments such as new guidance on the valuation of stocks, as well as the introduction of new accounting arrangements for capital.

Below is set out a list of the commercial Statements of Standard Accounting Practice (SSAP) and Financial Reporting Statements (FRS) as at June 1993 together with comments on their applicability to the NHS and, where appropriate a note that the standard is new. Where a previous NHS standard existed but has been amended, the entry is suffixed with an asterisk.

SSAP	Title	Comment
1	Accounting for associated companies	Not applicable
2	Disclosure of accounting policies	This statement is of fundamental importance and should be applied to accounts of the NHS*
3	Earnings per share	Not applicable
4	The accounting treatment of government grants (relates to grants made for purchase of fixed assets)	Not relevant as such, but suitable as the basis of an NHS standard to cover donations and donated assets (new standard)
5	Accounting for Value Added Tax	This standard is relevant to the accounts of the NHS
6	Extraordinary items and prior year adjustments	This standard has limited application to NHS accounts (see FRS3)
8	The treatment of taxation under the imputation system	Not applicable
9	Stocks and long term contracts	This standard is not relevant to the accounts of the NHS*
10	Statements of source and application	This standard is relevant to the account of the NHS* (see FRS1)
12	Accounting for depreciation	This standard is relevant to the accounts of the NHS (new standard)

13	Accounting for research and development	This standard has limited application to NHS accounts*
14	Group accounts	Not applicable (see FRS2)
15	Accounting for deferred tax	Not applicable
17	Accounting for post balance sheet events	This standard has limited application to NHS accounts
18	Accounting for contingencies	This standard is relevant to the accounts of the NHS
19	Accounting for investment properties	Not applicable
20	Foreign currency translation	This standard is relevant to the accounts of the NHS (new standard)
21	Accounting for leases and hire purchase contracts	Not applicable
22	Accounting for goodwill	Not applicable
23	Accounting for acquisitions and mergers	Not applicable
24	Accounting for pension costs	Not applicable
25	Segmental reporting	Not applicable
FRS		
1	Cash flow statements	Successor to SSAP10
2	Accounting for subsidiary undertakings	Successor to SSAP14
3	Reporting financial performance	Successor to SSAP6

Memorandum trading accounts

Trading and income and expenditure accounts in traditional commercial format are prepared in respect of eg. staff restaurants and canteens, hospital shops and farms and for accumulating and recharging the full cost of manufactured products.

These accounts are often organised to be profit-making at the gross profit stage, but result in a net deficit when overheads are taken into account. They may also be organised so that charged cover all costs, including an allowance for administration.

10 ♦ Final accounts and returns

The commercial format for canteen accounts would be as follows and, in addition, a balance sheet may be prepared.

	£	£		£
Provisions:			Sales	X
Opening stock	X			
Purchases	X			
	X			
Less: Closing stock	X			
		X		
Wages				
Kitchen	X			
Dining-room	X			
Cashier	X			
		X		
Gross surplus c/d		X		
		X		X

	£	£		£
Salaries and wages	X		Gross surplus b/d	X
National insurance and			Miscellaneous income	X
superannuation	X			
		X		
Electricity	X			
Gas	X			
Cleaning materials	X			
		X		
Printing and stationery	X			
Administration	X			
Repairs to equipment		X		
Laundry		X		
Provision for doubtful debt		X	Net deficit	X
		X		X

11

Charitable (trust) funds

Definition

'Trust Funds' (not to be confused with NHS Trusts), or 'Endowment Funds' are charitable, as distinct from Government or Exchequer funds. They derive from donations by individuals or organisations' or from legacies. Charitable funds for non-teaching hospitals were amalgamated to form the Hospital Endowments Fund in 1948 but this was redistributed in 1974 so that most Districts (and RHA's) now have a District (or Regional) General Fund. Trust Fund accounting is kept entirely separate from the remaining statutory accounts of the authority.

Powers

Health authorities have always had power to accept, hold and administer property on charitable trust. In 1980 they were given power to engage in fund raising activities. Considerable sums are also held on trust by other bodies for the benefit of particular health authorities or services, Leagues of Friends being one of the more common examples. An external trust should be registered as a charity and should not purport to represent the Authority.

Property and investments

Trust funds held by a DHA or a Trust are usually within one of the two following categories.

General purpose funds

Funds which are held without any externally imposed restriction other than the general obligation to use such funds for purposes relating to hospital services or research and which may be used at any hospital administered by or for which trustees have a responsibility.

Special purpose funds

Funds which are held for purposes specified by the donor or legatee. Such funds should only be applied for the specific purposes named in the trust instrument (ie. the letter enclosed with the donation, the Will etc). Specific conditions may indicate the hospital or ward on which the money must be used or the particular branch of the service which should benefit (eg. kidney transplants, heart disease etc).

The assets held on trust in the NHS have a value in excess of £600m. This includes both investments and property. In some cases the property has not been valued for many years and is probably worth much more. A very large proportion of the assets, particularly the property, is held by a comparatively small number of authorities, mainly teaching (undergraduate and postgraduate) hospitals. For most undergraduate teaching hospitals the trust funds are held by Special Trustees not the DHA.

Investments are managed by a variety of means. Funds are normally pooled so that only one single portfolio need to be maintained. Unless wider powers have been granted by the Charity Commissioners new monies added to an investment pool must be invested equally in wider (equity) and narrower (gilts) ranges as laid down in the *Trustee Investments Act 1961*. It is normal to appoint an investment adviser or manager who will be a member of one of the regulatory bodies approved by the SIB.

Income and expenditure

Income arises from gifts and legacies but also from property and investments or from fund raising. As the funds are charitable there is no tax liability.

Expenditure must be for the benefit of the services provided by the Authority and be in accordance with the purposes of the fund from which it is met. A very small number of funds are held on permanent endowment (described as Capital in Perpetuity in NHS accounts) so that only the income can be spent. For the rest of their funds Authorities have a policy on whether and to what extent capital should be expended. The only other restriction on how funds are spent is any prohibition set by the Secretary of State. The one standing restriction is not to use charitable funds to increase staff rates of pay.

Where the purposes of a gift (or a legacy) are specified by the donor it should be held in a 'Special Purposes' fund in order to be able to demonstrate that it has been spent accordingly. When it ceases to be possible to use this money for the purposes for which it was given the Charity Commissioners may be asked to make a 'Cy Pres' scheme to vary the purpose. This could apply if a hospital is closed or if a special purpose no longer exists.

Management

Whilst the whole Authority, as a corporate body, is the trustee of charitable funds it is normal to delegate the management to a small group of members to act on its behalf.

Charitable funds accounts

Separate accounts are maintained for Charitable Funds, comprising a balance sheet and income and expenditure account together with supporting notes. These are likely to be amended to comply with the Statement of Recommended Practice on Charities.

Proper books must be kept and the final accounts must be certified for authenticity by the appropriate treasurer. Trust fund balance sheets must comply with the Trustee Investments Act

1961. In addition the basis of the valuation of property must be identified, eg. original cost, professional valuation or insured value.

The accounts should show the main purposes for which trust funds, whether special or general, have been spent. Four usual categories are:

- amenities for patients;
- amenities for staff;
- research;
- other projects, including capital works and equipment.

Investments

Donations, legacies, dividends and interest received in any one year are unlikely to equal the demands made on trust funds in that year. Some years may see very large legacies and it may be considered desirable to spread the benefits over several years. Alternatively, it may be necessary to restrict the use of funds for several years in order to accumulate sufficient funds for a major project. For these reasons, trust funds generally have considerable surplus funds and these are either invested in fixed interest securities, shares or property to provide additional income.

The *Trustee Investment Act 1961* which applies to all NHS trusts, classifies investments as falling into three categories.

- Part I. Narrower range investments not requiring professional advice, for example National Savings Certificate, Defence Bonds, balances in a Trustee Savings Bank or the National Savings Bank;

- Part II. Narrower range investments requiring professional advice, for example government and local government stocks and bonds, fixed interest debenture stocks of certain UK companies, mortgages on UK land and so on;

- Part III. Wider range investments, all of which require professional advice, for example ordinary and preference shares of UK companies having over £1 million issued share capital and having paid a dividend on all their shares for the past five years. This category also includes other approved forms of equity holding, in particular unit trusts.

At least 50% of the funds invested must be in the narrower range. For accounting purposes, investments are shown as either 'narrow range' (combining Parts I and II) or 'wider range'. A health authority may have additional investment powers, awarded under a court order, or perhaps inherited under an ancient charter. Investments held under such powers are known as 'special range' investments and are shown in the balance sheet as a third category, after the narrower range and wider range figures.

Investments are carried in the balance sheet at book value, although market value is also disclosed.

Where investments have been revalued, the basis of valuation and all relevant details, such as the name and qualification of the valuer, must be disclosed.

Trust fund accounts

The accounts are prepared in the standard form laid down by the DH and consist of the following:

- An income and expenditure account.

- A balance sheet.

- Notes to the accounts, including the 'capital reserve – other funds and capital reserve – capital in perpetuity'. (The total accumulated income from all sources which remains unspent at the end of the year is recorded on the balance sheet under capital reserves. If the income was received with the condition that it be invested and only the interest spent, then it is recorded under 'capital reserves – capital in perpetuity'. This is referred to later in the chapter. All the other unspent income is recorded in the 'capital reserve – other funds' on the balance sheet.)

Income and expenditure account

The surplus or deficit for the year is calculated as the closing balance on the income and expenditure account. The account is prepared on an accruals basis.

The main features of the account are shown below.

Income and expenditure account: Health Authority Trust Fund

	£
Income	
Subscriptions and donations	X
Legacies	X
Dividends and interest	X
Net income from freehold and leasehold property	X
Income from fund raising	X
Other income	X
Net expenditure transferred to capital reserve – other fund*	X
Total income	X
Expenditure	
Administration expenses	X
Patients welfare and amenities	X
Staff welfare and amenities	X
Research	X
Contribution to hospital capital expenditure	X
Fund raising expenditure	X
Net income transferred to capital reserve – other fund*	X
Total expenditure	X

* Only one of these two entries will appear in the accounts, depending on whether there is more expenditure than income in the year or vice-versa.

Balance sheet

The balance on the 'capital reserve – other fund account' represents the total amount of the fund: the total amount which the trustees may spend on the services to patients and staff. At any one time most of this is held in the form of investments, but these may be sold to provide services to the extent of the 'other fund balance' if the trustees so wish.

If there has been an excess of income over expenditure in the current year then this amount will be added to the other fund balance in the balance sheet at the year end. If there has been an excess of expenditure over income on the other hand, then this will be subtracted, since the total amount of the fund has been reduced as a consequence of this year's activities.

The main features of the balance sheet are as follows:

Balance sheet: Health Authority Trust Fund

	£
Assets	
Property	X
Investments	
Narrower range (market value £X)	X
Wider range (market value £X)	X
Special range (including Charity Commission investment fund) (market value £X)	X
Stock in hand	X
Debtors	X
Cash in hand	X
Total assets	X
Reserves	
Capital reserves: funds held in perpetuity	X
General purposes	X
Special purposes	X
Capital reserves: other funds	
General purposes	X
Special purposes	X
Liabilities	
Sundry creditors	X
Cash overdrawn at bank	X
Total reserves and liabilities	X

Funds held in perpetuity and the distinction between general purpose and special purpose funds can be dealt with by notes to the Balance sheet.

Profit or loss on the sale of investments

If investments or property are sold for more than their book value then a profit is made. Since this occurs only occasionally and is not part of a regular annual income, it is not recorded in the income and expenditure account but is added directly to the 'other fund' account balance in the balance sheet. If there is a loss on the sale of investment or property, then the loss is deducted from the 'other fund' account balance.

Any profits or losses arising from the revaluation of property will be treated in the same way as those arising from the sale. Investments are shown at cost, but the market value at the year end will be disclosed by way of a note to the accounts. Property may be revalued on an *ad hoc* basis and the details of the revaluation will appear in the accounts.

NHS Charity review – Charities Act 1992

The *Charities Act 1992* amends the *Charities Act 1960* and introduces new legislation to maintain an up-to-date public register of charities. The NHS charity review had identified that existing records held by the Charity Commissioners are out of date and the aims of the review are four fold:

- to obtain up-to-date information about NHS charities;

- to encourage those acting as Trustees to use the small charities legislation contained in Sections 43 and 44 of the *Charities Act 1992*;

- to determine precisely how and what information should be entered on to the computerised register;

- to establish a registration timetable and procedure.

In addition to compulsory registration of charities, with appropriate penalties for non-compliance, a copy of the audited accounts of individual charities contained within trust funds will need to be submitted within a specified period to the Charity Commissioners each year.

Miscellaneous provisions allow the umbrella registration of very small individual charities, or those with very small income. Guidance and advice will continue to be given by the Charity Commissioners and the first set of annual accounts which need to be submitted to the Commissioners are understood to be those for 1994/95.

Both the Audit Commission and the HFMA are actively working with and cooperating with the Charity Commissioners in order to harmonise and consolidate the changes introduced in the *Charities Act 1992* and the subsequent NHS charity review.

Glossary of NHS financial terminology

The following terms are those specific to the NHS as set out in the NHSE Financial Management Training Initiative 'Basic Skills Training'.

Allocation
Share of cash limit that the District Health Authority must work within.

Block contract
The purchaser of health care pays an annual lump sum to the provider for a given level, type and quality of service, eg. a general service to a district. The nature of the service must be clearly defined.

Business Plans
Plans of action used by the Health Service in the 'post White Paper environment' containing three year rolling programmes which act as a control mechanism to ensure objectives are properly inter-related and realistic.

Capital charges
Costs of using capital (the estate, plus plant, equipment and vehicles). Charges are incurred by hospitals based on the capital they posses.

Capital expenditure
'Capital expenditure' relates to money spent on land, buildings and individual or groups of related items of equipment which are valued at more than £1,000 (increased to £5,000 on 1 April 1993) and have a useful life of more than one year. Routine maintenance of buildings is classified as revenue expenditure.

Capital funding
The sum of money allocated to RHAs and DHAs for the purpose of buying capital assets.

Capital items
Items to be charged to capital expenditure. In the post White Paper environment, this meant an asset or group of assets costing over £1,000 with a useful lifespan of more than one year (increased to £5,000 on 1 April 1993).

Capitation funding
Method of funding health authorities based on the health and age distribution of the resident population within an authority and the relative cost of providing services.

Case mix
The various group of treatments received by patients within a specialty (branch of medicine).

Clinical directors
A clinician who is responsible for the budgets of his own specialty or group of specialties.

Cost and volume contract
The purchaser pays an annual lump sum but there is an agreement that if additional services are required over and above the volume initially paid for, an additional charge is levied.

Cost per case contract
The purchaser negotiates an agreement with the provider on a patient by patient basis with no prior commitment by either party.

Cross accounting vouchers (CAVs)
Non-cash transfers of money between different health authorities (usually within the same Region), and often referred to as 'Inter-Authority Transfers'.

Cross boundary flows
The movement of patients across administrative boundaries for treatment.

DRGs
This stands for Diagnostic Related Groups and is the name given to a system of classifying acute, non-psychiatric in-patients according to their diagnostic characteristics and what treatment requirements they will need.

Family practitioner committees
Responsible for spending the primary care allocation outside health authorities (eg. spending on General Practitioners, local dentists and opticians).

Health service price index
A listing issued by the Department of Health which shows the monthly movement in prices of typical goods and services purchased by the NHS (ie. NHS version of the Retail Price Index).

Interest bearing debt
The current value of assets held by a hospital which is issued to calculate the interest element of capital charges payable to the Regional Health Authority for District Managed Units and the interest repayments from NHS Trusts to RHAs.

Internal market
This reflects the situation where Districts and Practice Fund holding GPs act as purchasers of health care services from providers clients. A District may purchase a service for a client from an NHS Trust or District Managed Unit in another part of the country as well as its local units.

Joint finance
Finance made available for projects relevant to both health authorities and local authorities.

NHS management executive
Senior management team at the DoH which implements the policies approved by the NHS Policy Board.

NHS policy board
Responsible for the overall NHS budget and strategic decisions facing the health service.

NHS trusts
Hospitals which do not come under the control of District Health Authorities but report direct to a Department of Health outpost (also referred to as Self-Governing Hospitals).

Overseas visitors
These are people not ordinarily resident in the United Kingdom who are charged for the provision of NHS treatment. Many patients who are overseas visitors will be exempt from payment through reciprocal arrangements with their country of origin and other clauses.

Providers of health care
Units of management responsible, under the White Paper, for providing health care within a geographical area. These include; directly managed hospitals (hospitals within Districts which do not seek self-governing status), NHS Trusts (self-governing hospitals), Private sector hospitals. The providers are those bodies with whom purchasers contract to provide health care services.

Purchasers of health care
Organisations and individuals who are responsible for buying health care from the providers in the light of the need of the population in a District or GP practice area. These include District Health Authorities and General Practitioners. Local authorities are the purchasers of health care in the community for the physically and mentally handicapped and elderly.

Referral patterns
When GPs ask for patients to be admitted to hospital they are referred to a medical consultant. Referral patterns show how recently and where certain types of patients are referred.

Special fund
Donations and legacies left to health authorities for specific purposes.

Special health authorities
Health authorities which provide specific, specialist health care services.

Specialty costing
Form of costing which apportions and allocates hospital costs to a particular branch of medicine (eg. paediatrics, orthopaedics, mental illness).

Specialty cost returns
Part of the Financial Returns which show patient care hospital costs allocated into particular branches of medicine.

Standing financial instructions
Financial rules and regulations for health authorities.

Strategic plan

Ten year programme showing the need for health services of an authority ranked in priority order.

Superannuation

This term refers to pensions in the NHS. The NHS Superannuation Scheme (NHSSS) is the health service pension scheme to which all staff who work full-time and are aged over 16 and part-time staff who work more than half the contracted hours of full-time staff are eligible to join.

Trust funds

All property received, held and administered by health authorities, or by any other bodies, for any purpose related to the NHS which does not originate from the Exchequer or is not an Exchequer responsibility.

Unit management

A division of management responsible for providing specific services within a health authority. Each unit is managed by a General Manager (UGM) who in turn reports to the District General Manager (DGM) of the DHA.

Questions

1 West Health Authority (D87)

The West Health Authority maintains a staff restaurant at the West Royal Infirmary (WRI). The following information is available for the year ended 31 March 19X7.

Balances at 1 April 19X6

			£
Stocks:	Provisions		3,345
	Cleaning materials		985
Creditors:	Provisions		4,086
	Gas		2,323
	Cleaning materials		880
	National Insurance		968
	Printing		98
Miscellaneous debtors			146
Cash float			30

Receipts and payments for the period

		£
Provisions		171,356
Salaries		7,654
Wages:	Kitchen	55,865
	Cashier	5,065
	Dining room	11,384
National Insurance and superannuation		13,985
Electricity		2,388
Gas		26,946
Laundry		3,441
Cleaning materials		1,064
Printing and stationery		460
Miscellaneous expenses		566
Sales		239,410
Miscellaneous receipts		1,932

Questions

The following amounts due to creditors at 31 March 19X7 have yet to be accounted for.

	£
Provisions	3,978
Gas	4,340
Electricity	780
Printing	28
National Insurance	1,578

The following information is also of relevance.

(1) The laundry service is provided by the hospital laundry and recharged through the year. The charge for the final quarter of 19X6/X7 is still outstanding and is expected to be at the same level as for the remainder of the year.

(2) At 31 March 19X7, provisions stocks amounted to £3,498 and stocks of cleaning materials to £324. However, £425 of provisions stocks are to be written off as unsaleable.

(3) Miscellaneous debtors amount to £248 at 31 March 19X7 but it is anticipated that one debt of £27 may be uncollectable.

(4) Space heating costs are recharged at the year end from the WRI on the basis of floor area. The following information is available.

WRI heating costs	£87,555
WRI floor area	17,511 square metres
Restaurant floor area	400 square metres

(5) The hospital also makes an administrative charge of £2,860.

(6) At 31 March 19X7 the float amounted to £18.

(7) The restaurant is not expected to break even. However, clear guidelines are laid down by the Health Authority:

   (i) prices should be set to cover cost of provisions consumed plus 50%;
   (ii) the deficit for the year must not exceed £50,000.

Required

(a) Prepare an income and expenditure account for the year to 31 March 19X7. (15 marks)

(b) Comment on the performance of the restaurant in view of the guidelines laid down by West Health Authority. (6 marks)

(c) Define each of the following and, by means of relevant examples, explain how they have been applied in answering part (a) of this question:

   – the matching concept;
   – the convention of conservativism;
   – the entity concept.

(9 marks)

(Total 30 marks)

2 Adun, Baran and Clede (J88)

Three health authorities, Adun, Baran and Clede, operate a joint computer consortium.

The following financial information is available.

Balances at 31 March 19X8

	£
Stocks of stationery	9,700
Cash balances	2,980
Creditor: Baran HA	12,680

Payments for the year to 31 December 19X8

	£
Rental of equipment	108,000
Salaries and wages	425,700
National insurance and superannuation	51,000
Maintenance	87,300
Transport	34,290
Stationery purchases	57,900
Electricity	34,780

Notes

(1) Average prices in the final quarter of 19X8/X9 are expected to be 2% higher than average prices in the first nine months of the financial year.

(2) An electricity bill amounting to £18,000 is unpaid at 31 December 19X8.

(3) A wage and salary award of 5% is to be implemented for all staff with effect from 1 January 19X9. National insurance and superannuation contributions may be expected to increase by a similar percentage from 1 January 19X9.

(4) The rental paid on equipment is paid quarterly, in arrears, at an amount fixed under a long-term agreement.

(5) Stocks of stationery at 31 December 19X8 amount to £14,800.

(6) The administrative expenses are borne by Baran HA and are recharged to the joint use facility at year end. For 19X8/X9 they are expected to amount to £88,000.

(7) Each of the three authorities make quarterly cash advances with respect to the scheme. The total advance each authority is to make in 19X8/X9 amount to:

	£'000
Adun HA	492.0
Baran HA	194.5
Clede HA	393.6

(8) The budgeted expenditure of the computer consortium for 19X8/X9 amounts to £1,180,000 at out-turn prices.

(9) Costs are apportioned to the three authorities based on usage. For 19X8/X9 it is confidently estimated that usage will be in the following proportions:

Adun HA	150
Baran HA	90
Clede HA	120

(10) Ditch HA has indicated that it wishes to discuss membership of the scheme: if it joins, stationery purchases are likely to increase by 30% and transport costs by 40%; its use of the facility is likely to be half that of Clede. There is, currently, sufficient spare capacity to accommodate Ditch.

(11) It is usual practice to round estimates to the nearest £10.

Required

(Note: Answer as at 31 December 19X8.)

(a) Prepare a statement indicating that estimated outturn expenditure of the computer facility for the year ended 31 March 19X9 and indicate how the net expenditure will be apportioned between the three health authorities. (15 marks)

(b) Prepare, in columnar form, the estimated personal accounts of the three health authorities for the year to 31 March 19X9. (6 marks)

(c) Prepare a brief note for the Joint Computer Services accountant indicating the financial implications of the entry of Ditch HA to the consortium with effect from 1 April 19X9.
(9 marks)
(Total 30 marks)

3 Central Health Authority (J90)

The following information relates to a trust fund account of Central Health Authority for the year ended 31 March 19X0. All transactions fall within the 'general purpose' category.

Balances at 1 April 19W9

	£
Property	55,000
Investments	204,560
Debtors	650
Creditors	1,135
Cash at bank	780
Stocks: welfare and amenities (patients)	1,200

Receipts and payments during 19W9/X0

Sale of investments		18,920
Net receipts from property		4,710
Donations received		16,500
Welfare and amenities payments		
Patients		12,918
Staff		4,874
Fund-raising expenses		435
Contributions to capital expenditure		4,400
Grants received		3,000
Fund-raising receipts		1,134
Purchases of investments		12,100
Dividend and interest received (net)		9,862
Contributions to support research		5,000
Miscellaneous receipts		321

Notes

(1) The opening debtors relate to investment income; £135 of the opening creditors refer to welfare and amenities payments for patients, the balance of opening creditors refers to purchases of investments.

(2) At 31 March 19X0, investment income of £1,340 was due.

(3) Income tax deducted at source from investment income and amounting to £2,543 is reclaimable from the Inland Revenue.

(4) Welfare and amenities (patients) stocks amount to £1,670 at 31 March 19X0, but on inspection stocks amounting to £565 are found to be out-of-date and are to be written off.

(5) Certain expenditure has been mistakenly charged to the Health Authority rather than to the trust fund; it amounts to £863.

(6) The investments sold during the year originally cost £15,680.

(7) Fund-raising creditors at 31 March 19X0 amounted to £85; fund-raising debtors amounted to £50, but, of this, £23 has been outstanding for more than six months and is to be written off.

(8) At 31 March 19X0, receipts from sales of investments totalling £1,300 are outstanding.

Required

(a) Prepare the income and expenditure account for the trust fund for the year ended 31 March 19X0.   (10 marks)

(b) Prepare the trust fund balance sheet as at 31 March 19X0.   (10 marks)

(c) You have been asked to reply to the following letter, on behalf of the Treasurer:

The Treasurer
Central Health Authority

25 May 19X0

Dear Sir

Health Authority accounts

I have just seen a copy of last year's accounts, and, being used to private sector accounts, the accounts of the Health Authority really do appear to be in a mess.

There appears to be no depreciation charge (!) and you appear to have excluded your assets, buildings, equipment, vehicles etc. from your balance sheet!

Could you enlighten me please?

Yours faithfully

K G Andrews

(10 marks)
(Total 30 marks)

4 Laundry (D89)

The following expenditure relates to a laundry maintained by the Cranbreak Health Authority for the eight months to 30 November 19X9.

	£
Employee costs	
Section manager	8,410
Superintendents	9,400
Laundry operatives	40,150
Administration	6,250
Other costs	
Washing materials	19,700
Water	4,880
Steam generation	8,800
Electricity	8,930
Rates	12,715
Transport	2,910
Miscellaneous	6,950

Statistics for the eight months to 30 November 19X9 show the following usage:

Number of articles processed   2,335,600

The following information is also to be taken into consideration.

(1) Managers and superintendents received a pay award of 7% with effect from 1 October 19X9. The increased payments for the months October and November are included within the above figures.

(2) All other employees will be awarded a pay increase of 6% with effect from 1 January 19Y0.

(3) Rates are payable on 1 April and 1 October. Both payments were made by the due date.

(4) Washing materials are expected to increase in price by 6% for the financial year as a whole.

(5) An electricity bill of £3,000 is estimated for the quarter to 31 December 19X9. The balances listed above include the payments for the first two quarters of the financial year. The bill for the January – March quarter is normally double the average bill for the remainder of the year.

(6) Analysis of 'miscellaneous expenditure' has revealed the inclusion of payments totalling £2,500 which should be charged to the medical care budgets of the authority.

(7) The laundry is expected to fully recover costs. To this end, the following budgets and charge-out rate for recovering costs were established in December 19X8 for the financial year to 31 March 19Y0:

Budgeted costs	£178,500
Estimated activity	3.5 million articles
Standard charge per article	5.1 pence

(8) Unless otherwise indicated, the pattern of expenditure and activity to 30 November 19X9 is expected to be typical of the pattern for the remainder of the year.

Required

(a) Prepare a statement showing estimated expenditure for the year to 31 March 19Y0.

(12 marks)

(b) Comment upon the laundry's financial performance for the year to 31 March 19Y0.

(10 marks)

(c) Indicate the principal users of the external financial reports prepared by health authorities, and their likely requirements with respect to the statements. (8 marks)

(Total 30 marks)

Questions

5 Chubb Health Authority (J91)

The following balances have been extracted from the accounts of Chubb Health Authority.

	Year ended 31.3.X0 £	Year ended 31.3.X1 £
Revenue expenditure		
Stock in hand	716,800	505,120
Deductions from salaries and wages not yet transferred	661,560	546,840
Debtors – Sundry	135,660	144,320
Creditors – Trade	522,380	476,840
– Sundry	276,460	303,700
Cash at bank		
In hand	35,840	
Overdrawn		46,930
Net revenue expenditure		64,310,900
Capital expenditure		
Creditors	395,680	478,910
Cash at bank	12,550	25,680
Net capital expenditure		3,200,080

The health authority has a cash limit for both capital and revenue expenditure and, through the year, it draws cash from the Department of Health, its total drawings in each category (capital and revenue) being compared with its cash limits.

Cash spending in excess of the cash limits must be carried forward and set off against the following year's allocation. Underspendings of up to 1% of the revenue cash limit and up to 10% of the capital cash limit may be carried forward. Any excess underspending will be lost to the authority.

Additionally, in any one year up to 1% of the revenue cash allocation may be transferred to capital and up to 10% of the capital cash allocation may be transferred to revenue.

Health authorities are required by the Department of Health to keep their cash balances as low as possible.

Chubb Health Authority had the following cash limit allocations for the year ended 31 March 19X1:

> Revenue cash limit: £63,958,130
> Capital cash limit: £4,064,900

Required

(a) Calculate the revenue cash out-turn and the capital cash out-turn for the year ended 31 March 19X1. (16 marks)

(b) Compare the figures calculated in (a) with the respective revenue and capital cash limits and, taking account of the transfer possibilities, draw conclusions from your comparison. (10 marks)

(c) Explain how the practice of 'brokerage' carried out by health authority treasurers may be of assistance to Chubb Health Authority. (4 marks)

(Total 30 marks)

6 Eastern Health Authority (J92)

The following information relates to a trust fund maintained by Eastern Health Authority for the year ended 31 March 19X2. All transactions fall within the 'General Purposes' category.

Balances at 1 April 19X1

	£
Property	44,000
Investments	163,200
Stocks: Welfare and Amenities (Patients)	1,120
Debtors	800
Bank	780 Dr
Creditors	1,240

Receipts and payments during 19X1 – X2

	£
Sales of investments	15,600
Net receipts from property	4,580
Donations received	13,200
Welfare and amenities payments	
Patients	10,333
Staff	3,900
Fund-raising expenses	348
Contributions to capital expenditure of HA	3,520
Grants received	2,407
Fund-raising receipts	907
Purchases of investments	9,680
Dividends and interest received (net)	7,890
Contribution made to HA to support research	4,000
Miscellaneous receipts	140

Notes

(1) At 31 March 19X2 receipts from sales of investments totalling £1,350 are outstanding; at the same date investment income totalling £506 was due.

(2) Income tax deducted at source from investment income and amounting to £485 is being reclaimed from the Inland Revenue.

(3) The opening debtors relate to investment income.

(4) The opening creditors figure refers to welfare and amenities payments for patients.

(5) Welfare and amenities (patients) stocks of food amounted to £1,670 at 31 March 19X2.

(6) The investments sold during the year had originally cost £12,100.

(7) Fund-raising debtors at 31 March 19X2 amounted to £51; fund-raising creditors at that date amounted to £34.

Questions

(8) A company in which shares were purchased some years ago has been subject to compulsory winding-up. The shares had cost £12,500 and had been recorded at that valuation at 1 April 19X1. They are now worthless.

(9) Welfare and Amenities (Patients) creditors amounted to £1,253 at 31 March 19X2.

Required

(a) Prepare the income expenditure account for the trust fund for the year ended 31 March 19X2.
(12 marks)

(b) Calculate the accumulated fund balance at 1 April 19X1 and prepare a Bank Account for the year ended 31 March 19X2. (4 marks)

(c) Prepare a trust fund balance sheet as at 31 March 19X2. (8 marks)

(d) Health authorities are in the process of devising procedures for charging depreciation on their assets for the first time. Outline *three* major problems that need to be overcome when any organisation moves to a system of depreciation for the first time. (6 marks)

(Total 30 marks)

7 East Grant Health Unit (D92)

The laundry service of the East Grant Health Unit is operated on an agency basis and is run on commercial accounting principles.

The financial management of the laundry service has been under the control of a manager who has suffered ill health for some time. The manager's absences have affected the smooth running of the accounting function and you have been asked to prepare the final accounts for the year ended 31 March 19X2.

The information at your disposal is as follows.

Balance sheet as at 31 March 19X1

Fixed assets	Cost £	Depreciation £	Net £
Plant and equipment	118,500	59,400	59,100
Vehicles	46,875	23,505	23,370
Fixtures and fittings	18,000	8,350	9,650
	183,375	91,255	92,120

Current assets			
Stock of materials	19,508		
Debtors	52,342		
Prepaid expenses	1,886		
Cash in hand	197		
		73,933	
Current liabilities			
Trade creditors	66,723		
Accrued expenses	3,157		
Bank overdraft	8,055		
		77,935	
			(4,002)
			88,118
			88,118

Capital: Reserves

Bank account summary for 19X1 – X2

	£		£
Receipts from debtors	564,938	Opening balance	8,055
Sale of vehicle	2,046	Payment to suppliers	331,934
		Laundry wages	74,911
		Expenses paid	59,533
		Drivers' wages	28,970
		Managerial salaries	27,955
		Purchase of vehicle	12,384
		Closing balance	23,242
	566,984		566,984

Your investigations reveal the following additional information.

(1) At 31 March 19X2 the outstanding debtors totalled £39,939 and suppliers of materials are owed £65,310.

(2) Accrued expenses at 31 March 19X2 are rent of £15,750, audit of £1,935, electricity of £14,314 and gas of £4,887.

(3) Payments in advance at 31 March 19X2 are rates of £745 and insurance of £1,299.

(4) The closing stock of materials at 31 March 19X2 was £7,337.

(5) Depreciation is to be provided as follows:

>   Plant 20% on cost
>   Vans 25% on written-down value
>   Furniture and fittings 15% on cost.

(6) During the year a driver was prosecuted for theft of materials costing £500. The insurance company has agreed the amount of the claim in full but has yet to pay the agency.

(7) Cheques drawn in payment for goods supplied but not yet presented to the bank at the year end totalled £1,440.

(8) The vehicle sold during the year had cost £12,128 and accumulated depreciation amounted to £8,075 at 31 March 19X2.

(9) Any cash shortfall may be assumed to relate to general expenses.

(10) Cash on hand at 31 March 19X2 amounted to £73.

Required

(a) Prepare a laundry profit and loss account for the year ended 31 March 19X2.   (16 marks)

(b) Prepare a balance sheet at 31 March 19X2.   (14 marks)

(Total 30 marks)

8 Reed Health Authority (J93)

Reed Health Authority maintains an occupational health unit (OHU) which has operated on a trading basis since 1 April 19X2. The unit provides an in-house service for Reed County Council under a long-established agreement. The agreement with the County Council has the following features.

(1) The Health Authority provides staff who are based at County Hall within accommodation provided by the County Council.

(2) The Health Authority provides an amount of free service as follows:

> | | |
> |---|---|
> | Pre-employment referrals | 100 |
> | Immunisations | 150 |
> | Other examinations | 100 |

(3) The County Council pays for any service in excess of this level.

The costs of the joint service for 19X2/X3 include the following elements.

(1) Direct staff costs incurred by the OHU:

Staff salaries	£46,000
Employer's NI	£3,860
Employer's superannuation	£4,140

(2) Drugs and dressings:

	£
Stock held at 1 April 19X2	2,451
Stock additions during year	3,990
Stock held at 31 March 19X3	2,550

(3) The office in County Hall occupies 15 square metres. Total office space at County Hall amounts to 600 square metres and the total costs of running this building during 19X2/X3 are as follows:

Running costs	£300,000
Financing costs	£200,000

The office is to bear a fair share of these premises costs.

(4) Telephone expenses of the office are borne initially by the County Council. The following details are available of the telephone bills paid by the County Council in respect of the telephone extension used by the OHU during the year ended 31 March 19X3.

For three months ended:

30 April 19X2	£57
31 July 19X2	£44
31 October 19X2	£63
31 January 19X3	£49
30 April 19X3	£39

The County Council has not been reimbursed for the last four bills itemised above.

(5) Travelling expenses are incurred by the OHU in respect of the County Hall service. At 1 April 19X2 a travelling claim of £43 was outstanding. During 19X2/X3 claims totalling £234 were paid and at 31 March 19X3 one claim of £20 was outstanding whilst an amount of £4 had been overpaid during the year and was being recovered from the employee concerned.

Actual levels of service provided by the County Hall based OHU during 19X2/X3 were as follows:

Pre-employment referrals	154
Immunisations	430
Visual display unit tests	45
Other examinations	284

Questions

The OHU, as indicated above, operates on a trading basis and its charges for the above types of activities were as follows during the year ended 31 March 19X3:

Pre-employment referrals	£44
Immunisations	£16.50
Visual display unit tests	£25
Other examinations	£44

(6) The Health Authority makes a global transfer of £15,000 to the OHU in respect of the 'free' element of service provided to the County Council.

(7) The OHU owes an amount of £615 to the County Council as at 1 April 19X2.

Required

(a) The manager of the occupational health unit wishes to determine the net cost of the County Council based service provision. Set up a trading account for this aspect of the unit's operation which will identify the net cost to the unit. (13 marks)

(b) Prepare Reed County Council's personal account as it would appear within the accounts of the occupational health unit and including all the relevant information. (5 marks)

(c) Comment on the situation disclosed by the trading account which you have prepared in part (a) and detail the action necessary to correct the position. (6 marks)

(d) Prior to April 19X2, Reed Health Authority spent time in developing a system of asset registers. Explain why this might have been necessary and draw up a list of headings which you would expect to find in an asset register. (6 marks)

(Total 30 marks)